ACHIEVING INTIMACY WITH JESUS CHRIST

A Study of the Four Gospels

Douglas M. Vincent

Judith E. Simms

authorHOUSE

AuthorHouse™
1663 Liberty Drive
Bloomington, IN 47403
www.authorhouse.com
Phone: 833-262-8899

Published by AuthorHouse 10/23/2024

ISBN: 979-8-8230-3669-6 (sc)
ISBN: 979-8-8230-3668-9 (e)

Library of Congress Control Number: 2024923388

Print information available on the last page.

This book is printed on acid-free paper.

*This workbook has been developed to assist Christians in achieving
a special intimacy with the Lord Jesus Christ.*

*All scriptures, unless otherwise indicated, are taken from the King James Version of the Holy Bible.
The words of Jesus appear like this sentence.*

Acknowledgements

God has placed several people in our paths that eagerly assisted us in many ways developing what you now hold in your hands. I want to acknowledge those individuals for their willingness to assist us.

I first want to acknowledge the co-author of this workbook, "Judi", for helping me develop this project and taking it to a whole new level. I thank her for her obedience in answering the call of Jesus Christ to publish *Achieving Intimacy With Jesus Christ*. She has worked long and hard at preparing a workbook that is accurate, with easy to read questions and scriptural support for every answer. I could never have done this without her genuine endeavor and relentless dedication.

Many people answered my plea for assistance in the early stages, before the idea to publish became a reality. As I wrote a few tests, God told me to start sharing them with those who didn't know Jesus Christ. I was obedient to the Lord's command and God sent them. I needed some people to help me produce more tests. I would like to thank Denise Sibert for typing and helping me get the first test ready for the new students. I would also like to thank Carrie Muldrow, who rendered much of her time typing and copying more new tests because the demand became greater to take the students to the next level.

Lastly, for all those whom I have not mentioned by name, I can never repay you for all that you have done. May God bless you richly and mightily!

Douglas M. Vincent

___

I would like to thank my co-author "Doug" for being an inspiration to me. I thank him for trusting me to do what God told me to do, which was "Publish It." Taking on this project has been an extremely eye-opening experience. God inspired Doug to create a workbook that anyone can use, along with his or her Bible, to achieve intimacy with Jesus Christ. If they truly desire to know Jesus, this workbook will challenge them to seek after Him. The Holy Spirit will reveal to them who Jesus really is and that *He is Love*.

I thank Yvonne Matthews for her dedicated assistance. She labored many, many hours proof reading this workbook. I thank God for her excitement, enthusiasm and availability as we forged ahead in producing this project. I owe much to you for the completion and success of *Achieving Intimacy With Jesus Christ*. May God continue to abundantly bless you and your family.

I also wish to express my heartfelt gratitude to my son, Theodore Simms, II, for his support throughout this entire process. He encouraged me when I needed it the most. He assisted in finalizing this workbook and, without him, this project would simply not be what it is. God Bless You - You're a Great Son!

Judith E. Simms

ACHIEVING INTIMACY
WITH JESUS CHRIST

TABLE OF CONTENTS

Part I: Study Questions for the Four Gospels (cont'd.)

Part II: Lesson Exam Questions for the Four Gospels

Part III: Final Exam Questions

Part IV: Memory Board and Pocket Scriptures

Preface
by Douglas M. Vincent

Achieving Intimacy With Jesus Christ was born out of tribulation. Let me explain. Five years ago, there were many things going on in my life that appeared to be more negative than positive. Two people, who were very important to me, died. I started questioning whether God was real. If he was real, then why did he allow these tragic events to occur? I asked him to reveal himself to me and show me that he was real. I accepted Jesus Christ as my Lord and Savior and made a commitment to give him my time. Then, I began to hear the voice of God.

In the midnight hour, God spoke to my spirit and said, "Let my people go." I responded, "Lord, your people are already set free – why are you bugging me?" Remember, at this point, I was a babe in Christ and was still working through some issues. He said that his people were physically free but not mentally or spiritually free. One of the first scriptures that God sowed into my spirit was the Old Testament Book of Hosea 4:6, which says, "My people are destroyed for lack of knowledge…" He said it is not all about church, but about His Word. He said his people have been following tradition for years. They come to the church, but not to God. They are not being renewed in their minds and need renovation on the inside, as well as the outside.

God said to me that most people don't have a personal relationship with him, but that I had stumbled upon this relationship through studying His Word. Then God instructed me to do something that I thought was really asking too much of me (don't forget that I was still very new in my relationship with Him). He told me to create a book that will allow his people to be transformed through the renewing of their minds. That was the command that brought this workbook into existence.

Of course, I really didn't want to do it. But God had already shown me that obedience is better then sacrifice. I did as God instructed. He told me to read the four gospels. Then, I was instructed to create questions that will encourage people to study His Word and develop an intimate relationship with Him. I was told to write ten questions for every three chapters of the entire four gospels. I was also instructed to choose scripture for the readers to commit to memory and deposit deep within their hearts. These scriptures will become vital tools that people will use in their daily Christian walk - especially when the trials of life occur. The Holy Spirit can bring that which is deposited in their hearts back to their memory. This book is written to encourage people to "Study to show thyself approved unto God, a workman that needeth not to be ashamed, rightly dividing the word of truth" (2 Timothy 2:15).

I want to thank God the Father, Jesus Christ the Son and the Holy Spirit for choosing, using, guiding and instructing me in the writing of this workbook. God gets all the glory, honor and praise because many lives will be changed by what is between the covers of this workbook.

Instructions For Using
Achieving Intimacy With Jesus Christ

As An Individual Teaching Aid

This workbook is centered on the Four Gospels of The Holy Bible. There are ten (10) study questions for every three chapters, beginning with the Gospel of Matthew and ending with the Gospel of John.

Begin your study with the Gospel of Matthew and repeat the following instructions for each of the remaining gospels.

1. *Complete the reading of all the scriptures* that are applicable to the Lesson that you will be studying before you answer the Study Questions for that Lesson. When you have completed your reading, *Answer the Study Questions.* You may refer back to the Bible to check to see that your answers are correct. (Note: Please refer to your Table of Contents to find the answers to all questions.)

2. Make sure that you *Memorize the Scripture Verses* for each Lesson before you proceed to the next Lesson.

3. After you have read the scriptures, answered the Study Questions and memorized the scripture verses for all nine (9) Lessons of the Gospel of Matthew, turn to page 103 and take the first exam for the Gospel of Matthew. Be honest with yourself and don't open your Bible. THIS IS NOT AN OPEN-BOOK TEST.

4. After you have completed all the Lessons for all four gospels and all four Lesson Exams, there is only one test left: the Final Exam. We know you can do it. Make sure you take time to prepare for this test by reviewing all the Lesson Study Questions and Lesson Exam Questions. Don't forget - "Study to show thyself approved…"

In A Classroom Setting

A teacher can easily develop a syllabus and lesson plans for a class that is based on this workbook. A deeper explanation of scripture and a greater emphasis placed on memorizing scripture will help to cultivate the information that students have already received in their reading. This workbook has thirty-eight (38) Lessons, four (4) Lesson Exams, and one (1) Final Exam. This workbook, on average, takes at least nine and a half months to complete in a classroom setting. You can also develop a schedule that will compress the program so that it may be completed in less time. But remember that memorizing the scripture verses is a very important aspect of this workbook. We want the student to memorize from the head and the heart. Lessons on the application of the Word are very effective in developing a strong Christian.

INTRODUCTION

ACHIEVING INTIMACY WITH JESUS CHRIST is a course created and designed to give you a better understanding of our Heavenly Father, our Lord and Savior Jesus Christ and the Holy Spirit. Jesus said, "I am the way, the truth, and the life: no man cometh unto the Father, but by me" (John 14:6). Jesus said, "Come unto me, all ye [you] that labor and are heavy laden, and I will give you rest. Take my yoke upon you, and learn of me; for I am meek and lowly in heart: and ye shall find rest unto your souls. For my yoke is easy, and my burden is light" (Matthew 11:28-30).

Jesus said, "I am the door: by me if any man enter in, he shall be saved, and shall go in and out, and shall find pasture" (John 10:9). The Bible states, "In the beginning was the Word, and the Word was with God, and the Word was God. The same was in the beginning with God. All things were made by him; and without him was not anything made that was made" (John 1:1-3). The scripture reads, "And the Word was made flesh, (and we beheld his glory, the glory as of the only begotten of the Father,) full of grace and truth" (John 1:14). "For the law was given by Moses, but grace and truth came by Jesus Christ. No man hath [have] seen God at any time; only the begotten Son, which is in the bosom of the Father, he hath declared him" (John 1:17-19).

Since Jesus Christ was with God in the beginning, we should learn what God has said through His Son. *Achieving Intimacy With Jesus Christ* will encourage you to eliminate *THE MIDDLE MAN*, such as scribes, Pharisees, hypocrites and even church tradition, and focus on **God's Word**. Makes sense, right?

This course focuses on the three most important characteristics that every person who seeks God must have:

1. You must have an intimate relationship with the Son (Jesus Christ).
   Read John 14:6.

2. You must be transformed or renewed in the spirit of your mind.
   Read Romans 12:2 and Ephesians 4:22-24.

3. You must be born again and become a new creature.
   Read John 3:3-8 and II Corinthians 5:17.

Continuing to read and plant scriptures from the four gospels (Matthew, Mark, Luke and John) in your heart will help you develop an intimate relationship with Christ. Jesus will strengthen you and teach you all the things the Father has taught Him. (John 17:6-8)

HELPFUL HINTS

We should thank God tremendously for sending us His Son Jesus Christ. Now, we have a **_method_** by which we can deal with the **_madness_** here on earth. Jesus said, "You believe in God, believe also in me" (John 14:1).

> *There are too many ways but only one,*
> *Too many days but what we have is none,*
> *Too many men but only through His Son.*
> *(Written by Douglas M. Vincent)*

In the parable of the sower, Jesus explains that the seeds are the word of God. (Luke 8:11-15) We know that seeds are meant to be planted. Jesus lets us know exactly where these seeds (the word) must be planted. They must be sown in our *hearts* as ammunition. If we don't deposit money in our checking account, we have nothing to withdraw. The same is true of His word. When the trials of life come against us and we have not planted the word of God in our hearts, we cannot make a withdrawal from the heavenly bank because the account is empty.

We must understand that our fight is a spiritual fight and, therefore, our weapons must also be spiritual. (2 Corinthians 10:3-5) In the parable of the sower, the seeds that fell on the *rock* represent the people that hear and receive the word of God with great joy, but *do not plant* the *word* in their *hearts.* In their time of trouble, they *panic* and *fall.* The *thorns* are those individuals that hear the word of God, begin *planting* the *word* in their *hearts,* and immediately begin to be blessed by God. Unfortunately, they *lose focus* of their primary agenda, which is *Jesus Christ* and growing to be *fruitful individuals.* They get *caught up* in the *blessing* and *not* the *Blesser* [who is God]. They soon get involved with the cares, riches and attention of people and the pleasures of this life.

Those seeds that fell on the *good ground* are individuals that have *good* and *honest hearts,* that *receive* the word of God, *hear it, plant it, keep it, and love it.* The good ground are those who *love God,* and not just His blessings. They remain humble and meek. They have a heart for God and are always abounding in the works of the Lord, even after being blessed by God. (2 Corinthians 15:58)

So, if we're going to become mighty men and women of God, we also need to learn how to fight the good fight of faith. We need to know that the word of God is *quick,* which means alive. It's *powerful* and *sharper* than any *double-edged sword* or any weapon that you could ever imagine. (Hebrews 4:12) David, a mighty man of God and a warrior for the kingdom of God, knew the importance of planting the word in his heart and *speaking life, not death,* over his circumstances and his problems.

David spoke life, which resulted in victory over the giant Goliath. David said, "Thou [You] comest [come] to me with a sword, and with a spear, and with a shield: but I come to thee [you] in the name of the Lord of hosts, the God of the armies of Israel, whom thou hast [have] defied. This day will the Lord deliver thee into mine [my] hand…" (I Samuel 17:45-46). Just as David spoke it and believed it - it happened. He defeated Goliath and took his head so that all the earth would know that there was a God in Israel. David knew the importance of *speaking* and *depositing* the word of God in his heart. It provided him with strength, protection and the ability to overcome temptation. David said, "Thy word I have hid in mine heart, that I might not sin against thee" (Psalm 119:11).

Jesus himself said, "…the words that I speak unto you, they are *spirit*, and they are *life*" (John 6:63). If the word adds life to us, then we need to have the word. Deuteronomy 30:14 says, "But the word is very nigh [near] unto thee, in thy [your] mouth, and in thy heart, that thou mayest do it." Are you ready to do it? To speak blessings not curses, to have *life* and not *death*, to have victory and not defeat? If you are ready to have these blessings and much, much more, then here are some materials you need to get started:

MATERIALS NEEDED

1) **Five (5) Sheets of Construction Paper:** Create your Memory Board.
2) **One Pack of Index Cards**: Tape or glue memory verses [found in the back of this workbook] onto index cards to be mounted on the Memory Board, or **One Small Pack of Cover Stock Copy Paper (67lb.):** Use a copy machine to duplicate the scriptures located in the back of this workbook. Mount them on your Memory Board. This same paper can be used to copy the pocket scriptures that you will carry with you and refer to while learning to memorize scripture.
3) **Tape or Glue and Scissors**: To cut-out and secure your scriptures to the construction paper.
4) **Bible**: Preferably the King James Version.
5) **Five Spiritual Books** listed below that will provide you with spiritual wisdom and guidance.

Now, the three (3) most important things that you will need are:
(a) A Humble Heart;
(b) A Desire to Have a Relationship with *God* the Father, His Son *Jesus Christ* and the *Holy Spirit*, and
(c) An Active Prayer Life.

ADDITIONAL READING MATERIALS

The books listed below will be beneficial to your spiritual growth:
1) UNDERSTANDING HOW TO FIGHT THE GOOD FIGHT OF FAITH: Kenneth E. Hagin
2) CRASHING SATAN'S PARTY: Dr. Millicent Thompson
3) PULLING DOWN STRONGHOLDS: John Osteen
4) THE BELIEVERS AUTHORITY: Kenneth E. Hagin
5) THE UNTAPPED POWER IN PRAISE: Kenneth Hagin, Jr.

Let these five books be a part of your spiritual library. They will provide you with some new strategies for living a godly life and will reveal to you a clearer understanding of the *treasure* and *power* that is inside of you. (II Corinthians 4:7, 4:16)

This course requires that you give God five (5) minutes a day in His word, not just in prayer. When you pray, God listens to you. But when you read, you listen to God. If God can stop His *busy schedule* to listen to you, then isn't it fair that you should take some time to listen to Him? Can you humble yourself daily, pick up your Bible, and give God five (5) minutes a day? Remember, Jesus said that if we are ashamed of Him now, He shall be ashamed of us then. (Luke 9:23-26)

If you have not confessed that Jesus Christ is your Lord and Savior, then please do so now. Just speak these words aloud: *Father God, I **confess** with **my mouth** the Lord Jesus and **believe** in my **heart** that you God have raised Him from the dead [come into my life Jesus and be my Lord and Savior, forgive me for my sins] in the name of Jesus. Amen! And now **I'm saved.*** (Romans 10:9-10) That's it. It's just that simple. Glory to God! Welcome Aboard. Now, begin learning to develop your prayer life. This can be done by reading and meditating on the Word of God, which are the scriptures. (Joshua 1:8-9)

Please note that in order for you to move through this course each week, you must complete the following:

A) Read five (5) minutes a day.
B) Complete the ten questions given for each week.
C) Meditate on the scriptures for that week.

D) Deposit the scriptures in your heart.
E) Be ready to recite the scriptures by heart memory.

Do not be **DISCOURAGED**. Remember what Jesus said, "When any one heareth the word of the kingdom, and understandeth it not..." (Matthew 13:19). Understand it how? Understand it *not*! He knows that you may not understand it in the *beginning*, but if you *continue* to seek *His word*, you will know the *truth* and the *truth* will set you free. If the Son Jesus makes you free, then you will be *free indeed.* (John 8:32, 8:36) *Glory to God!*

MEMORY BOARD

(EXAMPLE SHEET)

MATERIALS NEEDED
**Scissors, Glue or Tape,
Index Cards or One Small Pack of Cover Stock Copy Paper (67lb.),
Five (5) Large Sheets of Construction Paper,**

(STEP ONE) Take a sheet of construction paper and lay it on a flat surface. Cut out the Gospel of Matthew Header (found in the back of this workbook) and center it at the top of the paper. Attach with glue or tape.

(STEP TWO) Cut out Proverbs 18:21 [a Practical Eternal Truth (PET) Scripture] found in the back of the workbook. Center it directly below the Matthew Gospel Header.

Then, cut out Philippians 4:13 from the Matthew Memory Scriptures found in the back of the workbook. Place this scripture on the left side of the paper below the Proverbs scripture. Attach with either glue or tape *(See Example Below)*. These will be the first two scriptures you will learn for Week 1.

MATTHEW

| Proverbs 18:21 |
| PET Scripture – (Week 1) |

| Philippians 4:13 |
| (Week 1) |

(STEP THREE) Continue to add scriptures to your Memory Board **(one at a time)**, starting from week 2 through week 10 **(as you learn them)**. Once the left side of your Memory Board is filled, then add your verses to the right side.

(STEP FOUR) After completing the study of each gospel, your Memory Board should look like the illustration below. You should have **all 10 scriptures** on your Memory Board, as well as in your head and your *heart*. You now have ammunition for your battles. When they come - out of the abundance of the *heart*, *your mouth can speak*. Now, you can tell the storms what to do, like Jesus did. He said, "𝒫𝑒𝒶𝒸𝑒 𝒷𝑒 𝓈𝓉𝒾𝓁𝓁" (Mark 4:39). Now that's <u>power</u>! (Proverbs 18:21)

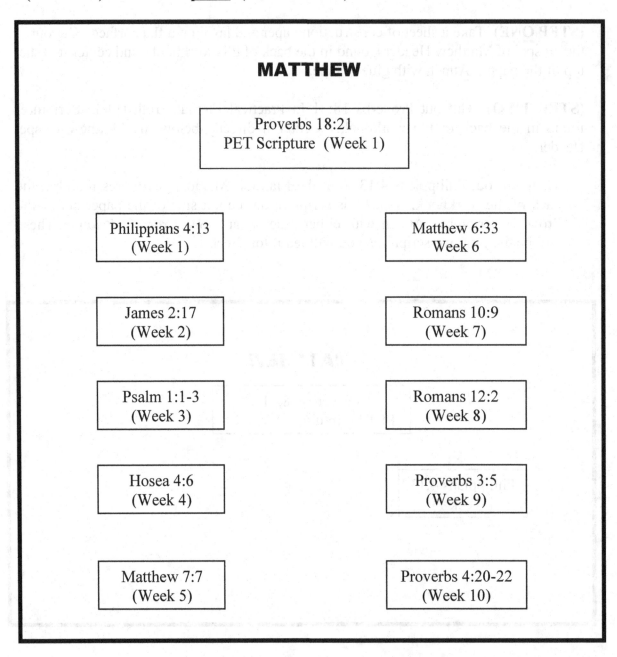

MATTHEW

Proverbs 18:21
PET Scripture (Week 1)

Philippians 4:13
(Week 1)

Matthew 6:33
Week 6

James 2:17
(Week 2)

Romans 10:9
(Week 7)

Psalm 1:1-3
(Week 3)

Romans 12:2
(Week 8)

Hosea 4:6
(Week 4)

Proverbs 3:5
(Week 9)

Matthew 7:7
(Week 5)

Proverbs 4:20-22
(Week 10)

❧ Practical Eternal Truth ❧

Memory Verses

We Challenge You!

In your lifetime, you will be thrown many curve balls. If you are anything like us, you have taken a hard swing at a few of them, only to realize that you shouldn't have tried to hit that last one. One key thing you must learn in this life is when to swing and when not to swing.

The Bible says, "There is a way which seemeth right unto a man, but the end thereof are the ways of death" (Proverbs 14:12). Listening and meditating on God's written word assures us of a home run each time life throws something us a curve ball.

In this workbook, you will find scriptures that will show you how to succeed in the challenges of life. The following nine pages are special thoughts on each memory verse for the nine lessons of the Gospel of Matthew. You are required to commit these verses to memory and hide them deep within your heart. We hope that you will be ignited with some motivating insight into the strength of God's Word.

We challenge you to write your own testimony or create your own motivating stories that focus on specific memory verses taken from the Gospels of Mark, Luke and John. You are required to create no less then 3 stories [one from each gospel] or as many additional stories as you wish from the remaining memory verses. There is something within you that God wants you to say. Pray and seek God for wisdom, knowledge and understanding in fulfilling this challenge. We hope that your thoughts will motivate others to study God's Word.

LESSON 1

Have you ever asked yourself any of these questions before: Can my life really be different? I'm tired and I really want to have a relationship with God, but can I? Can anything take me out of my life of drugs? How can I fight this depression? How do I break free from my homosexual behavior? How do I handle my big ego? How can I feel better about myself when I suffer from low self-esteem? Can I be faithful to anything or anyone? Where is my life going? What is my purpose in life? Am I equipped for life? Why can't I get ahead? I was never really good at reading the Bible, and there is so much that I don't understand – the spiritual and the natural part of life. Will I ever understand the Word?

I assure you that you can – and you will! God has promised:

I CAN DO <u>ALL THINGS</u> THROUGH <u>CHRIST</u>, WHO <u>STRENGTHENS ME</u>.
❧ Philippians 4:13 ❧
(NKJV)

Jesus Christ will be your answer. So, whenever these or any other questions enter your mind as to **HOW CAN I**, just remember that God has provided a way to strengthen you, to equip you, and to see you through.

LESSON 2

Have you ever placed your faith in a person, place or thing and found the outcome was not what you expected? OK – that's fine. Now *it's time* to place your faith in the One who made you, the One who came to earth to show you the way, the One who died for you, the One who knows you and loves you unconditionally. This is a very important time in your life.

You have spent *enough time* thinking and wanting. It's time *to do something!* Mentally desiring and wanting a change, without more, is not enough. Desire alone will get you nowhere. There must be some movement, some action, and some steps taken. In other words, some work must be done to give birth to the **NEW YOU,** that can't wait to get out. With a little faith (the size of a mustard seed), a little work and a little love, we can do all things. A little is a lot in the right hands. So place your hands in the hands of Jesus Christ. If you do these things, I assure you that *your life will be changed*. This brings us to our next verse:

EVEN SO <u>FAITH</u>, IF IT HATH <u>NOT</u> <u>WORKS</u> IS <u>DEAD</u>, BEING ALONE.
❧ James 2:17 ❧

He will equip you, lead you, and be with you, the entire way.
In the name of Jesus…

LESSON 3

You always hear people saying, "How are you doing?" Some respond, "I'm blessed." Wouldn't it be nice to know who is truly blessed by God?

Well, the word of God tells us, "Blessed *is* the man that walketh not in the counsel of the ungodly, nor standeth in the way of sinners, nor sitteth in the seat of the scornful. But his delight *is* in the law of the LORD [which is his word]; and in his law doth he meditate day and night. And he shall be like a tree planted by the rivers of water, that bringeth forth his fruit in his season; his leaf also shall not wither; and whatsoever he doeth shall prosper."

This particular scripture tells us that we are to *meditate* on God's word. It also reveals to us *when or how often* we should meditate. If we deal with this scripture as we would a prescription *(closely following* the **instructions**, *meditating* on His word a little in the **day** and a little at **night**), then the *Word* of God would be like **medicine.** It would quickly get inside of us and **clear up everything** on the inside, as well as the outside. Then, whatever you do, whatever you desire, whatever you touch, God has promised to prosper it.

BUT HIS DELIGHT IS IN THE LAW OF THE LORD; AND IN HIS <u>LAW</u> DOTH HE <u>MEDITATE</u> <u>DAY</u> AND <u>NIGHT</u>
❧ Psalm 1:1-2 ❧

LESSON 4

What is it that we're missing that is so terrible, so frightening, so important, so devastating, that it upsets and hurts our Lord and Savior, Jesus Christ? Have you ever heard people say, "If I had known then what I know now…"? God wants us to know His word before, not after, life's experiences have crushed us, hurt us, destroyed us, or caused bitterness in our hearts.

God Himself said in Hosea 4:6, "My people are destroyed for lack of knowledge…" The key point in this statement is that God said *His people*, not outsiders, *are destroyed* for their *lack of knowledge*.

If we can grab hold of God's word (his instructions, his laws, and his ways) early in life, and lean not to our own understanding, we will be successful and prosper. Jesus said it himself, "Man cannot live by bread alone, but by every word that proceedeth out of the mouth of God" (Math. 4:4). God truly loves us. He has done all the hard work for us. All we have to do is follow his lead, his steps, his program, and his word. It is our responsibility to go to the Bible and *find His wisdom, His knowledge, His understanding, and His love*.

Don't fall short. Don't let anything perish that God said you can have. People say what you don't know won't hurt you. God, our Creator, says…

MY <u>PEOPLE</u> ARE <u>DESTROYED</u>
FOR <u>LACK</u> OF <u>KNOWLEDGE</u>
❧ Hosea 4:6 ❧

LESSON 5

Isn't it funny how, when we talk with people and bring up the subject of God, they will often say to you, "Oh, I pray to God."

Well, that's good. Even Jesus prayed. In fact, Jesus said that men should always pray and faint not. Jesus also let us know, however, that prayer alone is not enough. If prayer was all that mankind needed, then the Father would not have sent Jesus. Jesus said, "I am the *way*, the *truth* and the *life*. No man cometh unto the Father, but by Me" (John 14:6). Jesus did three things while he was here on Earth. He expects us to follow Him and do the same three things. Following these steps will help us get through any situation or problem we may be experiencing.

Jesus knew that prayer alone, without works [movement] is dead. So, He came to show us that we must always be ready to move, be in position and continually practice His three-step program. A Step-Program is used to aid people who are in the process of *recovery*. Jesus Christ has given us a program to use so that we may recover and get back all that was stolen from us. Amen. The three-step program for Christians is called "*Ask, Seek, and Knock.*" *Ask* is when we earnestly and continually pray [inquire] to God with requests that are made in accordance with His will, which is His word. *Seek* is when we prayerfully, and with endeavor, look for those things we've asked of God. *Knock* is when we continue to be persistent, do not give up and diligently seek God. Jesus assures us that if we do this, the ***door will be open*** unto us.

Since we now know the truth, we must persevere. For the truth will set us free!

<u>ASK</u>, AND IT WILL BE <u>GIVEN</u> TO YOU;
<u>SEEK</u>, AND YOU WILL <u>FIND</u>;
<u>KNOCK</u>, AND THE DOOR WILL BE <u>OPENED</u> TO YOU.
Matthew 7:7

LESSON 6

Isn't it funny how the world is today? We live in a society that wants to dictate, as well as convince us of, *what's acceptable* and *what's not - what's successful* and *what's not.*   A fascinating quirk of humanity is when man will try to convince you of who you are, instead of *whose you are.* The world's idea of "success" will keep you continually reaching, striving, and pushing yourself to acquire *things* that will never *fulfill you*.

People allow money, jobs, material possessions, and even their outward appearance to become the most important factors in their lives. This type of success is not determined by God, but by man. It will keep you constantly focused on things that are outside the will of the Father. Then, you'll end up putting yourself first and God last. Thank God for His wonderful Son, our friend Jesus Christ, whom God sent to set the record straight. It's not that God doesn't want us to have these things and more. He does. But He wants us to attain them in the right manner. God loves us so much that Jesus said the *very hairs* of our head are *all numbered*. That's how closely He is watching us and how much He cares for us. God doesn't want us destroyed by our blessings. But He wants us happy, with our hearts focused on Him and being a blessing to others. When we *seek* after *God*, then we are *truly successful* and He becomes our reward, as well as our rewarder (Genesis 15:1).

God does not want us focusing all of our attention on acquiring worldly possessions. Instead, studying God's Word should be our first priority. If we put Him first, God will supply *all* our *needs* according to his riches in glory by Christ Jesus (Philippians 4:19). This brings us to our next verse:

**BUT <u>SEEK</u> YE <u>FIRST</u> THE <u>KINGDOM OF GOD</u>,
AND <u>HIS RIGHTEOUSNESS</u>; AND <u>ALL</u>
THESE <u>THINGS</u> SHALL BE <u>ADDED</u> UNTO <u>YOU</u>.**
❧ Matthew 6:33 ❧

LESSON 7

It is difficult for people to believe that God's desire is that no man should perish. We must keep in mind how powerful God is and that *His ways are not our ways, and His thoughts are not our thoughts.* (Isaiah 55:8-11) God knows our walk and He knows our fate. He knows that *human beings walk by sight* but the Holy Bible instructs us to *walk by faith and not by sight*. Faith is what you cannot see but believe God to accomplish for you.

If we are able to understand that God has made provision for us through His Son Jesus Christ, and has our best interests at heart, then our hearts and minds will be truly opened to better receive and understand the things that happen around and to us. Jesus said, "God so loved the world that He gave His only begotten Son, that whosoever believeth in Him should not perish, but have everlasting life" (John 3:16). Our whole existence and way of life is built on believing His Word.

God himself believed and then spoke saying, "Let there be light: and there was light" (Genesis Chapter 1:3). Everything that God created, He spoke it into existence. We are created in His image and likeness. We have the same rights and privileges as a child of God. It's not because of anything that we do, but through everything Christ has already done. Can you believe that God sent His Son to save you and me? If you can believe it, and say it, then you shall be saved. It's that simple! It's all done by faith. "For it's with the heart a man believeth unto righteousness and with the mouth confession is made unto salvation" (Romans 10:10).

**THAT IF YOU <u>CONFESS</u>
<u>WITH</u> YOUR <u>MOUTH</u> THE LORD JESUS,
AND <u>BELIEVE</u> <u>IN</u> YOUR <u>HEART</u>
THAT <u>GOD</u> HAS <u>RAISED</u> <u>HIM</u> FROM
THE DEAD, <u>YOU</u> WILL BE <u>SAVED</u>.**
❧ Romans 10:9 ❧
(NKJV)

LESSON 8

After a person has received salvation, one of the most important steps is for him or her to become more *Christ-like*. This is done by spending time in God's Word, developing a relationship with the Holy Spirit, and seeking God diligently in *prayer*. Many people attend church on Sunday. That is always a good thing. Unfortunately, they make no effort the rest of the week to attend *bible study, read their bibles, or develop a strong prayer life*. So what can we expect? If people knew the importance of the word of God and the power that's in the word, then they would understand God and how death or life can be in the power of their tongues. (Proverbs 18:21)

God has given us this world to have dominion over it. But first, we must be *transformed* before we can seize it. If we're going to become *salt* and *light* to a world that's in darkness, then we need to have our minds *renewed*. The Bible says a double-minded man (or woman) is unstable in all his (or her) ways. But, if we focus our minds on Christ, then we can and we will make a difference in this world. Are you ready to make a difference? Then, be ye transformed in the name of Jesus the Christ.

AND BE <u>NOT</u> <u>CONFORMED</u> TO THIS WORLD; BUT <u>BE</u> YE <u>TRANSFORMED</u> BY THE <u>RENEWING</u> <u>OF</u> <u>YOUR</u> <u>MIND</u>, THAT YOU MAY PROVE WHAT IS THAT GOOD, AND ACCEPTABLE, AND PERFECT, WILL OF GOD.
❧ Romans 12:2 ❧

LESSON 9

The Bible clearly tells you where true *wisdom, knowledge* and *understanding* come from. Proverbs, which is the book of wisdom, says, "The fear of the Lord is the beginning of wisdom…" (Proverbs 9:10). If we should fear the Lord, wouldn't it be prudent to know what we should fear about Him? Isn't it about time that we find out what God truly wants from us, and what it is that He truly loves about us? Are we going to continue missing our blessings, our inheritances, our rights, and our privileges, as a result of the *lack of knowledge?* Will we continue to *lean on our own understanding?* I hope not. Many people refuse to pick up the Bible and read it for various reasons: fear, intimidation, laziness, rebellion, and ignorance - just to name a few. II Timothy 3:16-17 says, "All scripture is given by inspiration of God, and is profitable for doctrine, for reproof, for correction, for instruction in righteousness: That the man of God may be perfect, thoroughly furnished unto all good works." We have a foundation. God has lovingly provided us with a guide and a better way of understanding who we are, whose we are and where we are in Christ Jesus. Isn't it about time that we are freed from bondage and the lack of knowledge?

Many people have not been properly trained to live a full life, especially when it comes to their spiritual life and relationship with Jesus Christ. Most often, people feel very uncomfortable when you ask them a question about God or about his word. Their response will vary from *Well, I feel; I think; I believe; I heard; and I suppose*; to *My mother said; My father said; My friend said; The Pastor said*. Well then, what did Jesus say? The answer is *"lean not to your own understanding"*. The devil himself got in big trouble when he planted in his heart and then spoke the word "I" (Isaiah 14:12-15). But Christ spoke what was written in the word of God and was exalted and freed from all bondage (Luke 4:1-15). The Bible says that a fool believes what he is told, but a wise man checks it out to see if it's true (Proverbs 14:15). We are going to need the Lord's help, direction and guidance if we're going to be *successful, prosperous,* and have heaven on earth (Deuteronomy 11:21). For in God's presence there is fullness of joy and at his right hand, pleasure for evermore (Psalm 16:11).

TRUST IN THE <u>LORD</u> WITH ALL YOUR <u>HEART,</u> AND <u>LEAN</u> <u>NOT</u> ON YOUR <u>OWN</u> <u>UNDERSTANDING</u>; IN ALL YOUR WAYS ACKNOWLEDGE HIM, AND HE <u>SHALL</u> <u>DIRECT</u> YOUR <u>PATHS.</u>
❧ Proverbs 3:5-6 ❧ (NKJV)

16

ACHIEVING INTIMACY
WITH JESUS CHRIST

STUDY QUESTIONS

FOR THE GOSPELS OF:

MATTHEW

MARK

LUKE

JOHN

Achieving Intimacy With Jesus Christ

Study Questions
Matthew Chapters 1 – 3

1. Was Mary pregnant before she married Joseph?

2. What type of man was Joseph?

3. Who told Joseph to marry Mary?

4. Why was Mary told to name the baby Jesus?

5. Did Mary and Joseph have sex before she had the baby?

6. The wise men came to worship Jesus when he was a child in Bethlehem. How did they find him?

7. Why didn't the wise men return home the same way they came?

8. Who told Joseph to take the baby Jesus and his mother and go into Egypt?

9. Why did King Herod want to know the location of the young child Jesus?

10. John the Baptist said, " I indeed baptize you with water unto your repentance: but He that comes after me is mightier than I, whose shoes I am not worthy to bear…" What are the two things the mightier one shall baptize you with? Who is John referring to?

_____

Write your PET scripture and the verse:

Proverbs _____

Write the scripture and verse for Lesson 1:

Philippians _____

Achieving Intimacy With Jesus Christ

Study Questions
Matthew Chapters 4 – 6

11. Who led Jesus into the wilderness to be tempted of the devil?

12. Who is the tempter and what false statement did he make when he tried to tempt the Son of God into proving himself?

13. What did Jesus continually and successfully use against the devil, which the devil tried to use against Jesus?

14. What did the devil offer Jesus if he would fall down and worship him?

15. Who ministered to Jesus when the temptation from the devil was over?

16. What substance should Christians be to the earth?

17. What are Christians to do that men may see their good works and glorify their father in heaven?

18. When you do something good, you should not brag or boast about it, nor sound a trumpet as hypocrites do. Why?

19. What did Jesus mean when he said, "...let not thy left hand know what thy right hand doeth..."?

20. Jesus said, "No man can serve two masters." Why?

_____

Write your PET scripture and the verse:

Proverbs _____

Write the scripture and verse for Lesson 2:

James _____

Achieving Intimacy With Jesus Christ

Study Questions
Matthew Chapters 7 – 9

21. Why should we not give anything holy, including ourselves, to the dogs?

22. If this world, being evil, knows how to give good gifts to their children, then our heavenly Father definitely knows how to give good gifts and much more to his children that do what?

23. For wide is the gate and broad is the way to what?

24. Beware of false prophets that come to you how?

25. How can we detect false prophets?

26. Whosoever does not build his spiritual wisdom, knowledge and understanding on the word of God is building his house on what?

27. A test of discipleship is for us to follow Jesus and let the dead do what for their dead?

28. Why did Jesus' disciples marvel at Him when the storm ceased?

29. What made the woman who touched Jesus' garment whole?

30. Jesus said the harvest is plenty. What was there a shortage of?

Write your PET scripture and the verse:

Proverbs _____

Write the scripture and verses for Lessons 1, 2 and 3:

Philippians _____

James _____

Psalm _____

Achieving Intimacy With Jesus Christ

Study Questions
Matthew Chapters 10 – 12

31. Jesus said that whosoever shall not receive you or the word of God, depart from that house and do what?

32. Not one sparrow shall fall on the ground without your Father knowing and the very hairs of your head are all numbered. Knowing this, we should not do what?

33. Jesus said, "Think not that I come to bring peace on earth…" Why did he come?

34. If we lack knowledge of the word, we are going to be sleeping with the enemy. Our enemies, our foes, and our adversaries are going to be of what?

35. When John was in prison and heard what Jesus was doing, he sent his disciples to ask him if he was the one to come or should they expect someone else? What was Jesus doing that John heard about?

36. John the Baptist was a messenger sent by the Father to do what?

37. Jesus said that from the days of John the Baptist until now, the kingdom of God suffers what?

38. Who did Jesus tell us to learn of?

39. Every kingdom, divided against itself, is brought to desolation. And every city or house, divided against itself, shall not what?

40. What happens when an unclean spirit is cast out of a man and he has not replaced the unclean spirit with the Spirit of God and God's Word?

_____

Write your PET scripture and the verse:

Proverbs _____

Write the scripture and verse for Lesson 4:

Hosea _____

Achieving Intimacy With Jesus Christ

Study Questions
Matthew Chapters 13 – 15

41. To whom is given the knowledge of the mysteries of the kingdom of heaven?

42. Where did Jesus say that the Word of God is sown?

43. What is the devil busy doing while we are learning the Word of God and depositing it inside of us?

44. He that is of the good ground hears the Word of God and does what?

45. Jesus did not do many mighty works in his own country or in his own house. Why?

46. What made Peter begin to sink when he walked on water to go to Jesus?

47. Jesus said that the people worshipped Him with their mouth and lips. How does Jesus want us to worship Him?

48. The Canaanite woman came to Jesus about healing her daughter. What was wrong with her daughter?

49. What did the Canaanite woman say to Jesus that revealed to Him her great faith?

50. Jesus had compassion on the multitude. Why?

_____

Write your PET scripture and the verse:

Proverbs _____

Write the scripture and verse for Lesson 5:

Matthew _____

Achieving Intimacy With Jesus Christ

Study Questions
Matthew Chapters 16 – 18

51. Jesus asked his disciples, "Whom do men say that I the Son of man am?" Which disciple answered him and what did he say?

52. Jesus said that he was going to build upon Peter. What did Jesus want to build?

53. Jesus said that we, as his disciples, have the keys to the kingdom of God. What should we be doing with the keys?

54. To whom did Jesus tell "Get thee behind me Satan…"? What did that person do wrong?

55. What are the three things Jesus said we should do if we are going to follow him?

56. Jesus took three of his disciples up into the mountain with him. Name the three disciples. Who appeared before their eyes? What did God say out of the clouds?

57. Jesus talked to Peter about casting a hook into the sea and catching a fish for what?

58. Jesus said that unless we do two things, we cannot enter the kingdom of God. What two things must we do?

59. Jesus said that if someone should offend one of the little children who believed in Him, it would be better if what would happen?

60. How often shall you forgive your brother if he offends you?

_____

Write your PET scripture and the verse:

Proverbs _____

Write the scripture and verses for Lessons 4, 5, and 6:

Hosea _____

Matthew _____

Matthew _____

Achieving Intimacy With Jesus Christ

Study Questions
Matthew Chapters 19 – 21

61. When a man is married, he should leave his father and his mother, be joined with his wife, and the two of them shall become what?

62. What God has joined together, let no man do what?

63. Why did Moses give a command of divorcement?

64. Under what circumstance did Jesus say divorce was acceptable?

65. Why did the rich young ruler go away sad after talking with Jesus about eternal life?

66. We as Christians should know that God will supply our needs. What did Jesus need that was in the village near Bethpage?

67. Why did Jesus start putting people out and turning over tables in the temple?

68. Why did Jesus curse the fig tree?

69. The stone that the builders rejected later became what? Jesus told the chief priests and the elders that the kingdom of God shall be taken from them, and given to a nation that will do what?

70. Whosoever shall fall, stumble, or trip on the stone shall be what?

Write your PET scripture and the verse:

Proverbs _____

Write the scripture and verse for Lesson 7:

Romans _____

Achieving Intimacy With Jesus Christ
Study Questions
Matthew Chapters 22 – 24

71. The Pharisees conspired how they might entangle Jesus by asking him about tribute to Caesar. What did Jesus say that amazed the Pharisees and caused them to leave?

72. The Sadducees came to Jesus with a question about the resurrection. What did Jesus say about their lack of knowledge?

73. What are the two greatest commandments?

74. What did Jesus say we should call no man on the earth?

75. What did the Scribes and Pharisees omit or neglect?

76. How did Jesus say the Scribes and Pharisees appeared?

77. What will all nations know before the end of the world comes?

78. Jesus said that even the very elect would be fooled. How?

79. When the Son of man comes in the clouds, He is coming with what? What is He sending forth?

80. Jesus said, "Heaven and earth shall pass away...." But what will remain?

_____

Write your PET scripture and the verse:

Proverbs _____

Write the scripture and verse for Lesson 8:

Romans _____

Achieving Intimacy With Jesus Christ

Study Questions
Matthew Chapters 25 – 28

81. In the parable of the ten virgins, five were wise and five were foolish. Please explain why they were wise and foolish?

82. When Jesus spoke of the parable of the talents, what did He say the lord of the servants said to the man with five talents and the man with two talents?

83. Jesus said that He would smite the shepherd and the sheep would do what?

84. Jesus was troubled in spirit and said that his soul was exceedingly sorrowful, even unto death. What did He ask his Father to do?

85. What was the sign that Jesus was the one to be arrested? What did Jesus call the disciple that betrayed him?

86. What did Jesus say about reaping and sowing that specifically pertained to the sword?

87. Pontius Pilate asked the multitude what he should do with Jesus. What did the people say and what did Pilate say after washing his hands?

88. In the parables of talents, God reveals that he never gives us less or more then we can handle. What did he say to reveal this?

89. Jesus said that our spirit is willing but what part of us is not willing?

90. How many times did Jesus catch his disciples asleep before he told them to sleep on?

Write your PET scripture and the verse:

Proverbs _____

Write the scripture and verses for Lessons 7, 8 and 9:

Romans _____

Romans _____

Proverbs _____

LIST OF MEMORY VERSES FOR MARK
LESSONS 1 – 5

The PET (Practical Eternal Truth) Scripture and Verse:

Genesis 1:26

The Scripture and Verse for:

Lesson 1: Matthew 28:18

Lesson 1: Luke 10:19

Lesson 2: John 1:12

Lesson 2: Romans 4:17

Lesson 3: Mark 16:17-18

Lesson 3: Mark 11:23-24

Lesson 4: Isaiah 54:17

Lesson 4: Psalm 121:1-2

Lesson 5: Psalm 61:1-2

Lesson 5: Psalm 105:14-15

Achieving Intimacy With Jesus Christ

Study Questions
Mark Chapters 1 – 3

1. Who was sent to prepare the way of the Lord?

2. How did Jesus get the unclean spirit out of the man?

3. Why did Jesus forbid the devil from speaking?

4. Why did the scribes say Jesus spoke blasphemy?

5. Why did Jesus eat and drink with the publicans and sinners?

6. When did Jesus say his disciples would fast?

7. Who was the Sabbath day made for?

8. Why did Jesus ordain his disciples?

9. The scribes said that Jesus cast devils out of people in whose name?

10. Who did Jesus say was his brother and his mother?

Write your PET scripture and the verse.

Genesis _____

Write the scripture and verses for Lesson 1.

Matthew _____

Luke _____

Achieving Intimacy With Jesus Christ

Study Questions
Mark Chapters 4 – 6

11. What does the sower sow?

12. Why does the devil come after us with affliction and persecution?

13. What should you take heed to?

14. What was the name of the unclean spirit that dwelled among the tombs?

15. Why did the people pray for Jesus to leave?

16. What did the ruler Jairus want from Jesus?

17. What healed the woman with the issue of blood?

18. What did Jesus say after Jairus was told his daughter was dead?

19. What did Jesus give his disciples before he sent them out to preach the gospel?

20. Who told Herod that he was unlawfully married?

Write your PET scripture and the verse.

Genesis _____

Write the scripture and verses for Lesson 2.

John _____

Romans _____

Achieving Intimacy With Jesus Christ

Study Questions
Mark Chapters 7 – 9

21. How did Jesus say the people honored him?

22. Why did Jesus reject the traditions of the elders?

23. What defiles a man?

24. Who did the people think Jesus was?

25. Who did Peter say Jesus was?

26. Why did Jesus rebuke Peter?

27. What two things did Jesus say this sinful generation should not be ashamed of?

28. What did Jesus tell the father, whose son had a dumb spirit, to do?

29. Why were the disciples unable to cast the dumb spirit out?

30. Why did Jesus tell his disciples not to forbid people that were casting out devils in his name?

Write your PET scripture and the verse.

Genesis _____

Write the scripture and verses for Lessons 1, 2 and 3.

Matthew _____

Luke _____

John _____

Romans _____

Mark _____

Mark _____

Achieving Intimacy With Jesus Christ

Study Questions
Mark Chapters 10 – 12

31. How should we receive the kingdom of God so that we may enter in?

32. Why was the rich young ruler grieved? What did the rich young ruler trust in?

33. When does God promise to bless us with a hundred fold?

34. What did the people say to the beggar, Bartimeus, about his voice? What did Bartimeus want from Jesus?

35. Why did Jesus send two of the disciples into the village?

36. What did Jesus do to curse the fig tree? Where did the fig tree start to wither?

37. What must we do to receive the things we desire and ask for in our prayers?

38. What did the chief priests, scribes and the elders want to know about Jesus' authority?

39. Why do people err when it comes to the things or the power of God?

40. What did the poor widow give that was more than all who cast money into the treasury?

Write your PET scripture and the verse.

Genesis _____

Write the scripture and verses for Lesson 4.

Isaiah _____

Psalm _____

Achieving Intimacy With Jesus Christ

Study Questions
Mark Chapters 13 – 16

41. Jesus said that you will hear of wars and rumors of wars, nations against nations, kingdoms against kingdoms, earthquakes in many places, famines and troubles. He also said that this was just the beginning. What did Jesus say must happen with the gospel before he returns?

42. In the last days, the Lord will shorten the calamity and chaos on the earth. Why?

43. What two types of people shall rise and do signs and wonders to seduce the people, even possibly the elect? Jesus forewarned us of all things to come. Why?

44. Where will Jesus appear and who will he have with him when He returns to earth after the Tribulation?

45. Jesus likens himself to a man who took a journey far away. What did the man give to his servants?

46. Jesus said, "...woe to that man by whom the Son of man is betrayed!" He said it would be better for this man if what?

47. What two things did Jesus tell Simon Peter to do so that he would not be tempted?

48. What did Jesus say when he was being accused of many things by the chief priests?

49. What six things did the soldiers do to mock [make fun of] Jesus?

50. What did Jesus commission his disciples to do after He had risen from the grave and appeared to them? What is it that should follow the believer?

Write your PET scripture and the verse.

Genesis _____

Write the scripture and verses for Lesson 5.

Psalm _____

Psalm _____

LIST OF MEMORY VERSES FOR LUKE
LESSONS 1 – 8

The PET (Practical Eternal Truth) Scripture and Verse:

II Corinthians 4:18

The Scripture and Verse for:

Lesson 1: Psalm 23:1

Lesson 1: I Peter 5:7

Lesson 2: Philippians 4:19

Lesson 3: I John 5:14

Lesson 4: Galatians 6:9

Lesson 5: Philippians 4:6

Lesson 6: Philippians 2:5

Lesson 6: James 1:8

Lesson 7: Isaiah 26:3

Lesson 7: Philippians 4:7

Lesson 8: II Corinthians 10:4-5

Lesson 8: Philippians 4:8

Achieving Intimacy With Jesus Christ

Study Questions
Luke Chapters 1 – 3

1. How did Zacharias and his wife Elisabeth walk before God?

2. What office did Zacharias hold and what was one of his duties?

3. What did Zacharias pray for and who told him that his prayers were answered?

4. What was John's job?

5. Why was Zacharias made dumb and unable to speak by Gabriel?

6. An angel came and told Mary that the Lord was with her and she was blessed among women. What did the angel say God had given her?

7. How was Mary going to conceive a child without knowing a man?

8. Who told the shepherds that Christ was born?

9. What was the Prophetess' name that visited the baby Jesus and gave thanks to God? How did the Prophetess serve God?

10. Where is the ax laid? What kind of tree is the ax laid against?

Write your PET scripture and the verse.

II Corinthians _____

Write the scripture and verses for Lesson 1.

Psalm _____

I Peter _____

Achieving Intimacy With Jesus Christ

Study Questions
Luke Chapters 4 – 6

11. How long was Jesus tempted by the devil?

12. What did the devil say he would give Jesus if he worshiped him?

13. In what country was Jesus not accepted?

14. Jesus told Peter to launch out into the deep and let down what for a draught or catch?

15. How many (answer to question #14) did Peter let down?

16. What was the result of Peter's disobedience (referring to the answer to question #15)? Name three other things that happened.

17. Why did Simon Peter tell Jesus to leave him?

18. What did Jesus say to the Pharisees and doctors of the law when healing the man sick with palsy?

19. What did Jesus say you should do to your enemies?

20. Who did Jesus say was Lord of the Sabbath?

Write your PET scripture and the verse.

II Corinthians _____

Write the scripture and verse for Lesson 2.

Philippians _____

Achieving Intimacy With Jesus Christ

Study Questions
Luke Chapters 7 – 9

21. Why did the centurion seek Jesus' help?

22. The centurion soldier felt unworthy to be in the presence of Jesus and for Jesus to enter under his roof. What did he have faith in? Jesus said the centurion had what kind of faith?

23. Who did Jesus say was greater than John the Baptist?

24. Why did the Pharisees and lawyers reject the counsel of God?

25. What is the seed called in the parable of the sower? What does the devil attempt to do with the seed?

26. Why did the people of Gadarenes want Jesus to leave?

27. How did Jesus know that the woman with the issue of blood touched him?

28. What did Jesus give his disciples before he sent them out to preach the kingdom of God?

29. Jesus told his disciples, "Take nothing for your journey...." What did he tell them to do if people would not receive the good news of the kingdom of God?

30. What did Jesus say we must do to follow him?

Write your PET scripture and the verse.

II Corinthians _____

Write the scripture and verses for Lessons 1, 2, and 3.

Psalm _____

I Peter _____

Philippians _____

I John _____

Achieving Intimacy With Jesus Christ

Study Questions
Luke Chapters 10 – 12

31. Jesus appointed disciples other than the main twelve and sent them out into every city. How many were appointed?

32. Jesus sent his disciples out and said, "Go your ways…." But what did He say about the lamb and the wolves?

33. What did Jesus say about those that hear the word and those that despise the word?

34. Why did the disciples return from the cities with great joy?

35. Jesus said to his disciples, "Behold, I give you power…." What kind of power did He give them?

36. What did Jesus tell the disciples they should rejoice over?

37. The people sought a sign from heaven. What did Jesus say their sign would be?

38. What did Jesus say he would do if you confess him before men?

39. What did Jesus say that you had to do to get the things you need?

40. When did Jesus say he would come?

_____

Write your PET scripture and the verse.

II Corinthians _____

Write the scripture and verse for Lesson 4.

Galatians _____

Achieving Intimacy With Jesus Christ

Study Questions
Luke Chapters 13 – 15

41. A certain man sought after fruit in the parable of the fig tree. What did he find? What did he tell the dresser [servant] to do to the tree?

42. Why was the woman bent over for eighteen years?

43. What does the kingdom of God resemble?

44. Jesus teaches on humility in the parable of the wedding feast. What should we do when we are invited to a feast that we may not be ashamed later? What will God do for us if we humble ourselves first in all that we do?

45. What did Jesus tell us to bear? What does Jesus tell us to count?

46. What do the three parables of the lost sheep, the lost coin and the lost son all have in common? Where is the joy found?

47. What did the son that was lost do with his portion of goods that his father gave him?

48. Why did the lost son find himself in need and unable to take care of himself?

49. What happened to the lost son after he thought about eating the husks that the swine ate?

50. What three words did the lost son speak that gave life to him, and moved him to get up and go see his father?

Write your PET scripture and the verse.

II Corinthians _____

Write the scripture and verse for Lesson 5.

Philippians _____

Achieving Intimacy With Jesus Christ

Study Questions
Luke Chapters 16 – 18

51. What did the unjust steward say when he was called to give an account of his stewardship? What was he ashamed to do?

52. Who was said to be wiser, the unjust children of his generation or the children of the light?

53. Where did the rich man and Lazarus go after they died? Who took them there?

54. What did the rich man receive in his lifetime and Lazarus in his lifetime? What did the rich man want for his tongue? Why?

55. Where is the kingdom of God located?

56. There is a parable about a widowed woman who wanted the judge to avenge her adversary. Why did the judge give into her?

57. What will God do for his own elect that cry out to him day and night?

58. Which man was justified in the parable of the two men who went into the temple to pray? Which one boasted about himself?

59. What happens when a person exalts himself and when a person humbles himself?

60. A certain ruler addressed Jesus as "Good Master." Who did Jesus say was good?

Write your PET scripture and the verse.

II Corinthians _____

Write the scripture and verses for Lessons 4, 5 and 6.

Galatians _____

Philippians _____

Philippians _____

James _____

Achieving Intimacy With Jesus Christ

Study Questions
Luke Chapters 19 – 21

61. Whose house did Jesus stay in when he entered Jericho? Why did the people murmur (complain)?

62. What instructions did the nobleman leave for his servants when he went into a far country to receive a kingdom for himself?

63. What did the nobleman want to know about the pounds that he had given his servants?

64. What did Jesus send his two disciples into the village to bring back?

65. What was hidden from Jerusalem's eyes that made Jesus weep?

66. Jesus said to the Pharisees that the days shall come when their enemies shall encompass them and be victorious. Why?

67. How did the scribes and the chief priests describe the way that Jesus taught?

68. How will the Son of Man come when he returns in the cloud to fulfill the word of God?

69. Heaven and earth shall pass away but what shall not pass away?

70. What two things did Jesus say we should do that we may be counted worthy to escape in the last day, when we shall see the Son of Man coming in a cloud?

Write your PET scripture and the verse.

II Corinthians _____

Write the scripture and verses for Lesson 7.

Isaiah _____

Philippians _____

Achieving Intimacy With Jesus Christ

Study Questions
Luke Chapters 22 – 24

71. What did the chief priests and scribes try to do to Jesus Christ at the Passover?

72. How were Peter and John to know the location of the house to be used for the eating of the Passover?

73. For who is greater in the kingdom of God, the person that sits at the table being served or the person that is doing the serving?

74. What did Satan desire to do to Simon Peter?

75. What did Jesus ask the Father to remove from him? Who appeared from heaven to strengthen Jesus during his trial?

76. On what side of God shall the Son of man be seated and what does it represent?

77. What saying did the people, rulers and soldiers repeatedly cry out?

78. Who was the man that asked for the body of Jesus?

79. When the women from Galilee arrived with their spices and ointment to the opened sepulchre of Jesus, they saw two men standing by them. Describe the men's garments. What did the men say about the living?

80. As the disciples returned to Jerusalem and were gathered together, talking about the Lord and how he appeared to Simon, Jesus stood in the midst of them. What were the disciples' reactions? What did Jesus say about a spirit?

_____

Write your PET scripture and the verse.

II Corinthians _____

Write the scripture and verse for Lesson 8.

II Corinthians _____

Philippians _____

LIST OF MEMORY VERSES FOR JOHN
LESSONS 1 – 7

The PET (Practical Eternal Truth) Scripture and Verse:

II Corinthians 5:17

The Scripture and Verse for:

Lesson 1: Hebrews 11:1

Lesson 2: Hebrews 11:6

Lesson 3: Romans 10:17

Lesson 4: II Corinthians 5:7

Lesson 5: Galatians 3:11

Lesson 6: Philippians 3:13-14

Lesson 7: Ephesians 4:22-24

Achieving Intimacy With Jesus Christ

Study Questions
John Chapters 1 – 3

1. Who was with God in the beginning?

2. "In him was life and that life was the light of men." What did that light do?

3. The Word was made flesh and lived where?

4. Moses brought the law. But what did Jesus Christ bring?

5. John the Baptist confessed that he was not the Christ, but was a voice sent to do what?

6. How did John the Baptist recognize that Jesus was the Christ?

7. To everything there is a season, a time and a purpose under the heavens. Did Jesus have to wait for his season before performing his miracles? What did he say to His mother at the marriage?

8. Why was Jesus so upset in the temple?

9. Who was the man that was a teacher, who came to see Jesus by night?

10. What must a man do to see or enter into the kingdom of God?

Write your PET scripture and the verse.

II Corinthians _____

Write the scripture and verse for Lesson 1.

Hebrews _____

Achieving Intimacy With Jesus Christ

Study Questions
John Chapters 4 – 6

11. Who was the woman at the well that Jesus asked to give him a drink?

12. Jesus said to the woman at the well that if she knew the gift of God, and who it is that is talking to her, she would ask and receive this gift. What is the gift?

13. Jesus said that the hour cometh when the true worshippers will worship the Father. How will they worship the Father?

14. What did Jesus say to the disciples when they wanted Him to eat something? What did he tell the disciples he had to complete?

15. Where did he say a prophet is not welcome?

16. What is the second miracle that Jesus performed? What did he say about signs and wonders?

17. Jesus knew the man at the pool of Bethesda had been waiting for the angel to trouble the water. The impotent man wasn't looking to be healed by Jesus. He was waiting for a man to do what?

18. The Jews were not concerned about the healing miracle of the impotent man. They were more concerned about the day on which Jesus healed him. Why?

19. Jesus said that he could do nothing of himself. What did he mean?

20. What type of bread did Jesus call himself? What must the Father do first before man can come to God?

Write your PET scripture and the verse.

II Corinthians _____

Write the scripture and the verse for Lesson 2.

Hebrews _____

Achieving Intimacy With Jesus Christ

Study Questions
John Chapters 7 – 9

21. To whom did Jesus say, "My time has not yet come..."?

22. A man that speaks of himself seeks his own what?

23. Jesus said that we should judge according to righteousness and not according to what?

24. They sought to take Jesus by force but no man laid hands on him. Why?

25. Jesus said that if any man thirsts, let him come unto him and drink. What will he receive?

26. The scribes and Pharisees said, "Master, this woman was caught in adultery, in the very act." What did Jesus say that amazed them and made them walk away one-by-one?

27. What will we be if we continue in Jesus' Word? What will happen?

28. He that is of God hears God's what?

29. The man that was blind from birth was blind for what reason?

30. The blind man told the Jewish leaders that he didn't know whether Jesus was a sinner or not, but all he knew was what? He also said that God did not hear the prayers of sinners, but the prayers of whom?

_____

Write your PET scripture and the verse.

II Corinthians _____

Write the scripture and verses for Lessons 1, 2, and 3.

Hebrews _____

Hebrews _____

Romans _____

Achieving Intimacy With Jesus Christ

Study Questions
John Chapters 10 – 12

31. Who are they that enter not by the door? How does the shepherd of the sheep enter?

32. Name three ways the sheep can detect a good shepherd?

33. What do the sheep do when they encounter a stranger?

34. In order for us to live and have green pastures, we need to go through what door and become what?

35. What does a thief come to do? What does the good shepherd come to do?

36. Who is it that cares not for the sheep?

37. Who died that caused Jesus to weep and how many days was he in the grave?

38. Jesus said, "Take ye away the stone" [from the grave]. Who came forth when Jesus spoke with a loud voice and what did Jesus say about the grave clothes?

39. Many people came to Bethany not only to see Jesus, but also to see whom? What did they want?

40. What did Jesus say about a corn of wheat that dies? What did he say about being lifted up?

_____

Write your PET scripture and the verse.

II Corinthians _____

Write the scripture and verse for Lesson 4.

II Corinthians _____

Achieving Intimacy With Jesus Christ

Study Questions
John Chapters 13 – 15

41. Who did the devil enter into that betrayed Jesus?

42. Who was the disciple that resisted having his feet washed by Jesus?

43. What did Jesus tell Peter he must do if he wanted to be a part of his ministry?

44. Jesus said "… love one another; as I have loved you…." What commandment is this?

45. What is the only way we can come unto the Father?

46. How are we to pray or ask the Father for anything and get it?

47. Why can't this world receive the Comforter? What kind of spirit is He?

48. Who is the comforter? What does He come to do?

49. If Jesus is the true vine and God is the husbandman [gardener], then what are Christians? What should they be doing? When are they cast away?

50. What is the greatest act of love that man can do? Why would the world hate you?

_____

Write your PET scripture and the verse.

II Corinthians _____

Write the scripture and verse for Lesson 5.

Galatians _____

Achieving Intimacy With Jesus Christ

Study Questions
John Chapters 16 – 18

51. If you were spreading the gospel [the good news], why would people want to put you out of places or hurt you, thinking that they are doing the right thing?

52. Why was it expedient or to our advantage that Christ leave? What did this mean to the world?

53. What will the Spirit of Truth do when he comes?

54. What did Jesus leave with you that no man can take from you? What are you to do with it that it may be fulfilled?

55. Why did Jesus say be of good cheer?

56. Jesus said that he prayed not for the world. Who was Jesus praying for? Who do they belong to?

57. Jesus said that they are not of this world and the world hates them. Who is Jesus referring to? What did he give them that would make the world hate them?

58. Where did Jesus often go with his disciples to rest?

59. Who is the only person that fought for Jesus upon his arrest? How did he fight?

60. What does Jesus own that is above and not of this world? What was He born to be in that world?

Write your PET scripture and the verse.

II Corinthians _____

Write the scripture and verses for Lessons 4, 5, and 6.

II Corinthians _____

Galatians _____

Philippians _____

Achieving Intimacy With Jesus Christ

Study Questions
John Chapters 19 – 21

61. What kind of crown did the soldiers place upon the head of Jesus? What color was Jesus' robe?

62. After the soldiers dressed Jesus and greeted Him as a king, what did they do next?

63. Pilate said that he could find no fault in Jesus, but the Jews wanted Him crucified. Why?

64. Who told Jesus that he had the power to crucify him or to release him? What did Jesus say?

65. What was the title placed on Jesus' cross by Pilate?

66. Who were the three women that stood by the cross of Jesus?

67. After Jesus said, "I thirst" and "It is finished," what did he give up?

68. Who was the first person to see Jesus after he arose from the grave? This person ran to share the good news with the disciples.

69. Who was the disciple that doubted the resurrection of Jesus? What is the only way he would believe?

70. What did Jesus tell Peter to do three times if he truly loved him?

_____

Write your PET scripture and the verse.

II Corinthians _____

Write the scripture and verse for Lesson 7.

Ephesians _____

ACHIEVING INTIMACY WITH JESUS CHRIST

LESSON EXAM QUESTIONS

FOR THE GOSPELS OF:

MATTHEW

MARK

LUKE

JOHN

Achieving Intimacy With Jesus Christ

EXAM #1
GOSPEL OF MATTHEW

1. What did John the Baptist say was "at hand" when he preached in the wilderness of Judea?

2. Christians are to be flavor to the earth. What flavor or substance should they be?

3. What three words did Jesus use to fight the devil?

4. Jesus said that when we pray, we should pray in secret and God would reward us how?

5. Jesus said, "No man can serve two masters." Why?

6. What are Christians to do so that men may see their good works and glorify their Father in Heaven?

7. Jesus said that foxes have holes and birds have nests, but he had nowhere to do what?

8. Jesus said that we should learn of someone. Who?

9. Jesus explained that we should call no man on earth, only God, by this title?

EXAM #1
Gospel of Matthew

10. Why did Peter begin to sink when he walked on the water towards Jesus?

_____

MULTIPLE CHOICE

11. Jesus came to do what to the law?
    A. Destroy the law
    B. Change the law
    C. Be the law
    D. Fulfill the law

12. When does God know that we need something?
    A. The minute we ask
    B. After we ask
    C. Before we ask
    D. As soon as we ask

13. Jesus said that not everyone who calls him Lord shall enter into the Kingdom of God. Who shall enter?
    A. The praisers
    B. Those who pray
    C. Those who repent
    D. The obedient

14. What was Jesus doing in the boat before he calmed the sea?
    A. Teaching the disciples
    B. Preaching to the crowd
    C. Fishing with the disciples
    D. Praying to His Father
    E. Sleeping in the ship

15. Jesus told the disciples that He was sending them out as sheep in the midst of wolves. He told them to be as wise as what?
    A. Doves
    B. Foxes
    C. Owls
    D. Sheep
    E. Serpents

EXAM #1
Gospel of Matthew

TRUE OR FALSE

16. A man's enemy shall be they of his own household.

    True   False

17. Jesus thanked God for hiding the truth from the wise.

    True   False

18. Jesus said, "Heaven and earth shall pass away but I shall remain."

    True   False

19. Jesus told the disciples that he would be with them until the end of the world?

    True   False

20. The devil tempted Jesus by offering him the kingdoms of the world.

    True   False

BONUS QUESTIONS

21. What are the two greatest commandments?

    A.

    B.

EXAM #1
Gospel of Matthew

22. To be the greatest in the Kingdom of God, you must:
  A. Be obedient
  B. Be a servant
  C. First seek the kingdom
  D. Trust in the Lord and lean not to your own understanding

23. All sins are forgiven, except suicide.

  True or False

24. When Jesus rose - we rose. Whatever Jesus has - we have. Whatever Jesus can do - we can do and greater. What is the one thing the devil could do to Jesus and he is allowed to do to us?

25. People worship God with their mouths. How does God want us to worship Him?

MATTHEW – FOUNDATION SCRIPTURES

WRITE THE NINE (9) SCRIPTURES LISTED BELOW.

► **WEEK #1   (PET SCRIPTURE)**
    PROVERBS _____ :

► **WEEK #1**
    PHILIPPIANS _____ :

► **WEEK #2**
    JAMES _____ :

EXAM #1
Gospel of Matthew

▶**WEEK #3**
   PSALM _____ :

▶ **WEEK #4**
   HOSEA _____ :

▶**WEEK #5**
   MATTHEW _____ :

▶**WEEK #6**
   MATTHEW _____ :

▶**WEEK #7**
   ROMANS _____ :

▶**WEEK #8**
   ROMANS _____ :

▶**WEEK #9**
   PROVERBS _____ :

Achieving Intimacy With Jesus Christ

EXAM #2
GOSPEL OF MARK

1. John the Baptist preached, saying, "There cometh one mightier than I after me, the latchet of whose shoes I am not worthy to stoop down and unloose. I indeed have baptized you with water..." But he shall baptize you with what?

2. Jesus met two fishermen, Simon and Andrew. He told them to follow him and gave them a new job. What was their new occupation?

3. When Jesus came to the country of Gardarenes and stepped out of the boat, a man possessed with an unclean spirit met Jesus. This man could not be tamed or bound. Where did he live?

4. What was the possessed man doing to himself physically before he met Jesus and how did he appear after Jesus healed him?

    A.

    B.

5. Jesus commanded the unclean spirit to come out of the man. Jesus asked him, "What is thy name?" What did the unclean spirit say?

6. Jesus immediately felt healing power gone out of him and turned toward the crowd and said, "Who touched my clothes?" Who was it that touched Jesus and was healed?

EXAM #2
Gospel of Mark

7. Jairus, a ruler of the Synagogue, had a dying daughter and sought Jesus greatly for his little daughter's life. When Jesus arrived at Jairus' place, he inquired about the commotion and crying. What comment did Jesus make that caused them to laugh at him?

8. The rich young ruler asked Jesus, "Good Master, what shall I do that I may inherit eternal life?" Jesus said, "...go thy way, sell whatsoever thou hast, and give to the poor, and thou shalt have treasure in heaven: come take up the cross, and follow me." What was more important to the young ruler than eternal life?

9. What are the first and second most important commandments of them all?

10. Jesus said that whatsoever you say, you shall have it. But you must do two important things. What are those two things?

MULTIPLE CHOICE

11. Who came and ministered to Jesus after he had been in the wilderness for forty days and was tempted by Satan?
    A. His disciples
    B. The Samaritan woman
    C. God
    D. Some people
    E. Angels
    F. The Holy Spirit

EXAM #2
Gospel of Mark

12. What defiles a man?
    A. What he eats
    B. What he sees
    C. What he touches
    D. What he thinks
    E. What is in his heart
    F. What he puts in his body

13. The Disciples couldn't cast out an unclean spirit. But Jesus said that all things are possible if you believe. Who said, "Lord, I believe"?
    A. The possessed man
    B. The possessed mother
    C. The father of possessed child
    D. The disciples

14. Jesus prepared his disciples and sent them out. How?
    A. Two by two
    B. With power over all clean spirits
    C. With no money
    D. With no food
    E. All of the above

15. The chief priests and scribes sought how they might take Jesus and put him to death, but not on the feast of the Passover. Why?
    A. Because of God
    B. The laws
    C. Because of Jesus' power
    D. Fear of possible uproar of the people
    E. All of the above

16. What descended upon Jesus when he was baptized and had come up out of the water?
    A. The angels
    B. The voice of God
    C. The rain
    D. Melodies from Heaven
    E. Bread from Heaven
    F. The Holy Spirit

EXAM #2
Gospel of Mark

TRUE OR FALSE

17. Jesus said, "How hard [difficult] will it be for people who have riches to enter into the Kingdom of God!"

True   False

18. If any man desires to be great, he must concentrate on himself first and believe that all things are possible to him that believes.

True   False

19. When it comes to being tempted, Jesus said that if your hand offends you (causes you to sin), you should cut it off.

True   False

20. There's no man that has left his earthly possessions or family to follow Jesus that will not be given a hundred fold in return.

True   **False**

BONUS QUESTIONS

21. Jesus said, "Whosoever therefore shall be ashamed of me and of my words in this adulterous and sinful generation; of him also shall the Son of man be ashamed, when he cometh in the glory of his Father with the holy angels." Explain what Jesus meant.

22. Who will the Son of man send and whom will he gather when he comes to glorify His Father?

EXAM #2
Gospel of Mark

23. John said, "Master, we saw one casting out devils in thy name, and he followeth not us: and we forbad him, because he followeth not us." But Jesus said, "Forbid him not..." Why?

24. Jesus said that the people honored Him with their lips and worshipped Him in vain laying aside the commandment of God.   What didn't people honor Him with that Jesus said was far away from Him?

25. The Sadducees raised a question about resurrection with regard to a woman who was married seven times. They wanted to know whose wife she would be in the next life. What did Jesus say?

MARK – AUTHORITY / POWER SCRIPTURES

WRITE THE TWELVE (12) SCRIPTURES LISTED BELOW.

▶ **WEEK #1   (PET SCRIPTURE)**
   GENESIS _____ :

▶ **WEEK #1**
   PROVERBS _____ :

EXAM #2
Gospel of Mark

▶**WEEK #1**
 MATTHEW _____:

▶**WEEK #1**
 LUKE _____:

▶**WEEK #2**
 JOHN _____:

▶**WEEK #2**
 ROMANS _____:

▶**WEEK #3**
 MARK _____:

EXAM #2
Gospel of Mark

▶**WEEK #3**
  MARK _____:

▶**WEEK #4**
  ISAIAH _____:

▶**WEEK #4**
  PSALM _____:

▶**WEEK #5**
  PSALM _____:

▶**WEEK #5**
  PSALM _____:

Achieving Intimacy With Jesus Christ

EXAM #3
GOSPEL OF LUKE

1. An angel talked to Mary and told her that she had found favor with God. Favor to do what?

2. Mary said to the angel, "How shall this be, seeing I know not a man?" How will she conceive?

3. What did the baby in Elisabeth's womb do when Mary greeted Elisabeth?

4. Who was Elisabeth the mother of and who was Mary's son?

   A. _____

   B. _____

5. Jesus laid hands on the sick and they were healed. Devils also came out. Why did Jesus forbid the demons to speak?

6. Jesus was tempted in the wilderness by the devil for forty days. What did he eat?

EXAM #3
Gospel of Luke

7. Jesus was told that his mother and brethren desired to see him. What did Jesus say?

8. Jesus said that when you are converted or become a Christian you should do what to your brothers and sisters in Christ?

9. A man said to Jesus, "I besought thy disciples to cast out an evil spirit, but they couldn't." Why?

10. Jesus said, "Judge not, and ye shall not be judged: condemn not. and ye shall not be condemned: forgive, and you shall be forgiven...." Then he said we could have good things, pressed down, shaken together and running over. What must we do?

11. A centurion soldier, who understood what authority meant, wanted his servant healed. He said that he was not worthy of meeting Jesus, but knew that when Jesus spoke the word, his servant would be healed. What did Jesus see in this man that was so great and not found in all of Israel?

12. Jesus fed a multitude of people that followed him. What did he feed them with?

13. Jesus said that if any man desired to come after him, they must do what?

EXAM #3
Gospel of Luke

MULTIPLE CHOICE

14. **How were Mary and Elisabeth related?**
    A. Friends
    B. Cousins
    C. Sisters
    D. Step-Sisters

15. **Why did Mary and Joseph sleep in the manger?**
    A. They had no money
    B. They were on the run
    C. They had followed a star there
    D. They was no room available

16. **The disciples asked Jesus to increase their faith. What did he say?**
    A. Be obedient
    B. Pray without ceasing
    C. Be a servant first
    D. Have faith as a grain of mustard seed
    E. Be watchful and pray

17. **What will the Holy Spirit help us to do when we are being persecuted or going through trials and tribulations?**
    A. Lay hands on those who persecute you
    B. Hide from the problems
    C. Call fire down from heaven
    D. Teach us in the same hour what to say
    E. All of the above

TRUE OR FALSE

18. **An unclean spirit led Jesus into the wilderness.**

    True   False

19. **Judas betrayed Jesus with a friendly hug.**

    True   False

EXAM #3
Gospel of Luke

20. Jesus told Peter that he would deny Him before the cock crowed three times.

        True   False

BONUS QUESTIONS

21. What did Jesus see in the men that lowered their friend who had palsy through the housetop where Jesus was teaching?

22. How old was Jesus when his parents left him in Jerusalem thinking he was with family and friends?

23. Later, Jesus' parents returned to Jerusalem and found Him doing what in the temple?

24. What did Jesus say to his parents when they found him in the temple?

25. Jesus said. "Let the dead bury their dead…" What did Jesus want us to do?

EXAM #3
Gospel of Luke

LUKE – COMFORT SCRIPTURES

WRITE THE THIRTEEN (13) SCRIPTURES LISTED BELOW.

►**WEEK #1   (PET SCRIPTURE)**
  II CORINTHIANS _____:

►**WEEK #1**
  PSALM _____:

►**WEEK #1**
  I PETER _____:

►**WEEK #2**
  PHILIPPIANS _____:

►**WEEK #3**
  I JOHN _____:

►**WEEK #4**
  GALATIANS _____:

►**WEEK #5**
  PHILIPPIANS _____:

EXAM #3
Gospel of Luke

LUKE – MIND SCRIPTURES

▶ **WEEK #6**
   PHILIPPIANS _____:

▶ **WEEK #6**
   JAMES _____:

▶ **WEEK #7**
   ISAIAH _____:

▶ **WEEK #7**
   PHILIPPIANS _____:

▶ **WEEK #8**
   II CORINTHIANS _____:

▶ **WEEK #8**
   PHILIPPIANS _____:

Achieving Intimacy With Jesus Christ

EXAM #4
GOSPEL OF JOHN

1. In the beginning was the word, and the word was with God, and the word was
   God, and the word became flesh, and dwelt among us. Who is the word?

2. What was Jesus' first miracle? What did He say to his mother before doing the
   miracle?
   A.

   B.

3. He came to his own but his own received him not. What did he do for those who
   received him?

4. That which is flesh is flesh and that which is spirit is spirit. What must we do to
   become spirit?

5. For God so loved the world he gave his only begotten son. Why?

6. Jesus testified that a prophet is not welcome where?

7. Jesus says that no man can come to him, except when the Father does this to the
   man?

EXAM #4
Gospel of John

8. No man laid hands on Jesus while he was preaching. Why?

9. Jesus said that he who enters not by the door, but climbs up some other way, is what?

10. Jesus said, "I am the good shepherd...." The good shepherd does something the hired shepherd won't do. What?

11. Why was Lazarus sick?

12. Why did the chief priests want to kill Lazarus, whom Jesus raised from the dead?

MULTIPLE CHOICE

13. How many days was Lazarus in the tomb?
    A. Three days
    B. Four days
    C. Five days

14. Why did the Pharisees fear the Lord Jesus?
    A. Because of the miracles
    B. Because he raised Lazarus
    C. Because men believed in him
    D. Because he was the Son God

Achieving Intimacy With Jesus Christ   **Page 3**

EXAM #4
Gospel of John

15. Jesus said that in his Father's house there are what?
    A. A place for you
    B. The way
    C. Life
    D. Many mansions

16. Why did Jesus wash his disciples' feet?
    A. Because it was the last supper
    B. To expose the traitor
    C. To be an example of what they should do
    D. Because their feet were dirty

17. What did Jesus say about joy?
    A. It shall come to pass
    B. Watch and pray that it comes
    C. It is the substance of things
    D. No man takes it away

TRUE OR FALSE

18. No man hath ascended to heaven but Jesus.

        True   False

19. Jesus called himself the prince of this world.

        True   False

20. Jesus did not trust men because he knew what was in them.

        True   False

BONUS QUESTIONS

21. What is God's job description?

83

EXAM #4
Gospel of John

22. What is Jesus' job description?

23. What is the job of the Holy Ghost?

24. What is the job of a Christian?

25. What is Satan's job?

26. What will the water that Jesus gives do for you?

27. How shall the true worshippers worship the Father?

28. Jesus said that if we truly love him, we would do what?

JOHN – FAITH SCRIPTURES

WRITE THE EIGHT (8) SCRIPTURES LISTED BELOW.

▶**WEEK #1   (PET SCRIPTURE)**
   II CORINTHIANS _____:

EXAM #4
Gospel of John

▶**WEEK #1**
  HEBREWS _____:

▶**WEEK #2**
  HEBREWS _____:

▶**WEEK #3**
  ROMANS _____:

▶**WEEK #4**
  II CORINTHIANS _____:

▶**WEEK #5**
  GALATIANS _____:

▶**WEEK #6**
  PHILIPPIANS _____:

▶**WEEK #7**
  EPHESIANS _____:

ACHIEVING INTIMACY WITH JESUS CHRIST

FINAL EXAM QUESTIONS

FOR THE GOSPELS OF:

MATTHEW

MARK

LUKE

JOHN

Achieving Intimacy With Jesus Christ

FINAL EXAM
The Four Gospels

1. Why did Jesus tell Mary not to touch Him after he had been resurrected?

2. What did Jesus say to the Pharisees and Scribes about the woman who was caught in the act of adultery?

3. Jesus said that we are truly His disciples and we would know the truth and be made free if we do what?

4. What did Jesus say is the truth?

5. How did Jesus tell us to come to His Father?

6. Jesus told Peter to do something for Him. Three times he repeated this to him. What did he say?

7. Jesus knows everything before it happens. What is the one thing Jesus, the Son of God, said He didn't know?

8. Which disciple doubted the resurrection of Christ?

9. Jesus said, "All ye shall be offended because of me this night, for it is written I will smite the shepherd," and what did he say the sheep will do?

10. Jesus gave a parable of the ten virgins. He said that five were wise and five were foolish. What made the five virgins foolish?

11. Jesus said that wide is the gate and broad is the way that leads to what?

12. How many times did Jesus find His disciples asleep when he was praying in the Garden of Gethsemane? What did He continue to say to them?

13. Jesus gave an example of what happens when a person joins with another person. He said that a man should leave his father and mother and shall cleave to his wife and the two of them shall become what?

14. What is the shortest scripture in the Bible, which describes the way Jesus felt about Lazarus' death?

15. The Bible said that Jesus often experienced a certain emotion for the people. What was this?

16. The Pharisees asked Jesus if it was lawful to give tribute to Caesar or not? Jesus said, "Whose is this image and superscription?" The Pharisees responded, "Caesar's." What was Jesus' response?

17. What was the crown made of that was placed by the soldiers on the head of the King of Glory?

18. In the parable of the talents, what did the lord of the servants say he would do to the men who were faithful over a few things?

19. When Pilate said that he had the power to crucify Jesus or to release Him, what did Jesus say?

20. Name six things other than beating Him that the soldiers did to Jesus before they nailed Him to the cross?

21. What three words did Jesus use in response to the devil's temptations?

22. Jesus said that when we pray, we should pray in secret and God would reward us how?

23. Jesus said, "No man can serve two masters..." Why?

24. What are Christians to do that men may see their good works and glorify their Father in Heaven?

25. Jesus said that we should learn of someone. Who?

26. Jesus said that, because only God is worthy, no man on earth should be called by what title?

27. Why did Peter begin to sink as he walked on the water toward Jesus?

28. "In the beginning was the Word, and the Word was with God, and the Word was God, and the Word became flesh and dwelled among us." Who is the Word?

29. "That which is born of the flesh is flesh; and that which is born of the Spirit is spirit." What must we do to become spirit?

30. Jesus said that no man can come to him, except the Father does what to the man?

31. Jesus said, "He that enter not by the door but climbs up some other way..." is what?

32. Jesus said that He was the good shepherd. What does the good shepherd do that the hired shepherd won't do?

33. Why was Lazarus sick?

34. Jesus was told, "Thy mother and brethren desire to see you." What did Jesus say?

35. Jesus said that when you become a Christian, you should do something very specific to your brothers and sisters in Christ. What must you do?

36. A man said to Jesus, "I besought thy disciples to cast out an evil spirit, but they couldn't." Why?

37. Jesus said that if any man desired to come after Him, he must do what?

38. Jesus met two fishermen, Simon and Andrew, and told them to follow Him. He gave them a new job. What was their new occupation?

39. What was the possessed man (having an unclean spirit that could not be tamed or bound) physically doing to himself before he met Jesus?

40. Jesus said that whatever you desire, you shall have it. What two things must you do to have what you desire?

MULTIPLE CHOICE

41. Jesus said, "Not everyone that says Lord, Lord, shall enter into the kingdom of God." Who shall?
    - ☐ **The praisers**
    - ☐ **Those who pray**
    - ☐ **Those who repent**
    - ☐ **The obedient**

42. Jesus said, "Behold, I send you out as sheep in the midst of wolves...."
    Christians should be wise as:
    - ☐ Doves
    - ☐ Foxes
    - ☐ Owls
    - ☐ Sheep
    - ☐ Serpents

43. **Why did the Pharisees fear the Lord Jesus?**
    - ☐ Because of the miracles
    - ☐ Because He raised Lazarus
    - ☐ Because men believed in Him
    - ☐ Because He was the Son of God

44. **What did Jesus say about joy?**
    - ☐ It shall come to pass
    - ☐ Watch and pray that it come
    - ☐ It's the substance of things
    - ☐ No man take it away

45. **The disciples asked Jesus to increase their faith. What did He say they should have?**
    - ☐ Obedient spirit
    - ☐ Prayer without ceasing
    - ☐ Servant's attitude
    - ☐ Faith as a grain of mustard seed
    - ☐ Reprobate mind

46. **What defiles a man?**
    - ☐ What he eats
    - ☐ What he sees
    - ☐ What he touches
    - ☐ What he thinks
    - ☐ What is in his heart
    - ☐ What he puts in his body

TRUE OR FALSE

47. A man's enemy shall be they of his own household.

☐ True   ☐ False

48. Jesus said, "Heaven, earth and my words shall pass away."

☐ True   ☐ False

49. Judas betrayed Jesus with a friendly hug.

☐ True   ☐ False

50. Jesus told Peter, "You will deny me before the cock crows three times."

☐ True   ☐ False

SCRIPTURES

I. WRITE-IN WHERE THESE SCRIPTURES ARE FOUND.

51. I can do all things through Christ who strengthens me. *(NKJV)*

Chapter & Verse: _____

52. *Ask, and it shall be given you; seek, and ye shall find; knock, and it shall be opened unto you:*

Chapter & Verse: _____

53. That if you confess with your mouth the Lord Jesus, and believe in your heart that God raised Him from the dead, you will be saved. *(NKJV)*

Chapter & Verse: _____

54. Now faith is the substance of things hoped for, the evidence of things not seen.

Chapter & Verse: _____

55. (For we walk by faith, not by sight:)

    Chapter & Verse: _____

56. Brethren, I count not myself to have apprehended: but *this* one thing *I do*, forgetting those things which are behind, and reaching forth unto those things which are before, I press toward the mark for the prize of the high calling of God in Christ Jesus.

    Chapter & Verse: _____

57. That ye put off concerning the former conversation the old man, which is corrupt according to the deceitful lusts; And be renewed in the spirit of your mind;

    Chapter & Verse: _____

58. The LORD *is* my shepherd; I shall not want.

    Chapter & Verse: _____

59. But my God shall supply all your need according to his riches in glory by Christ Jesus.

    Chapter & Verse: _____

60. And the peace of God, which passeth all understanding, shall keep your hearts and minds through Christ Jesus.

    Chapter & Verse: _____

61. A double minded man *is* unstable in all his ways.

    Chapter & Verse: _____

62. Finally, brethren, whatsoever things are true, whatsoever things *are* honest, whatsoever things *are* just, whatsoever things *are* pure, whatsoever things *are* lovely, whatsoever things *are* of good report; if *there be* any virtue, and if *there be* any praise, think on these things.

    Chapter & Verse: _____

63. No weapon that is formed against thee shall prosper; and every tongue *that* shall rise against thee in judgment thou shalt condemn. This *is* the heritage of the servants of the LORD, and their righteousness *is* of me, saith the LORD.

    Chapter & Verse: _____

64. Hear my cry, O God; attend unto my prayer. From the end of the earth will I cry unto thee, when my heart is overwhelmed: lead me to the rock *that* is higher than I.

    Chapter & Verse: _____

65. All power is given unto me in heaven and in earth.

    Chapter & Verse: _____

66. But as many as received him, to them gave he power to become the sons of God, *even* to them that believe on his name:

    Chapter & Verse: _____

67. And these signs shall follow them that believe; In my name shall they cast out devils; they shall speak with new tongues; They shall take up serpents; and if they drink any deadly thing, it shall not hurt them; they shall lay hands on the sick, and they shall recover.

    Chapter & Verse: _____

II. FILL IN THE BLANKS OF THIS SCRIPTURE

68. For verily I say unto you, That whosoever shall _____unto this mountain, Be thou _____, and be thou cast into the sea; and shall not _____ in his _____, but shall _____ that those things which he saith shall come to pass; he shall have whatsoever he saith. Therefore I say unto you, What things soever ye _____, when ye _____, believe that ye _____ *them*, and ye shall _____ *them*.

III. WRITE THE COMPLETE SCRIPTURE VERSE

69. MATTHEW 6:33

_____

_____

_____

70. ROMANS 12:2

_____

_____

_____

71. PROVERBS 3:5-6

_____

_____

_____

72. JAMES 2:17

_____

_____

_____

73. HEBREWS 11:6

_____

_____

_____

74. ROMANS 10:17

_____

_____

_____

75.   II CORINTHIANS 5:17

_____

_____

_____

76.   I PETER 5:7

_____

_____

_____

77.   I JOHN 5:14

_____

_____

_____

78.   PHILIPPIANS 4:6

_____

_____

_____

79.   PHILIPPIANS 2:5

_____

_____

_____

80.   ISAIAH 26:3

_____

_____

_____

81.   **II CORINTHIANS 10:4-5**

_____

_____

_____

82.   **PSALM 121:1**

_____

_____

_____

MEMORY
BOARD
SCRIPTURES

&

POCKET
SCRIPTURES

MEMORY BOARD HEADERS

MATTHEW

MARK

LUKE

JOHN

MEMORY BOOK HEADERS

MATTHEW

MARK

LUKE

JOHN

PROVERBS 18:21

Death and life are in the power of the tongue:
and they that love it shall eat the fruit thereof.

Matthew - PET Scripture

- ✂ -

PHILIPPIANS 4:13

I can do all things through Christ
who strengthens me.   *(NKJV)*

Matthew - Lesson 1

- ✂ -

JAMES 2:17

Even so faith, if it hath not works,
is dead, being alone.

Matthew - Lesson 2

PSALM 1:2

**But his delight is in the law of the LORD; and
in his law doth he meditate day and night.**

Matthew - Lesson 3

- ✂ - - - - - - - - - - - - - - - - - -

HOSEA 4:6

**My people are destroyed for lack of knowledge: because
thou hast rejected knowledge, I will also reject thee,
that thou shalt be no priest to me: seeing
thou hast forgotten the law of thy God,
I will also forget thy children.**

Matthew - Lesson 4

- ✂ - - - - - - - - - - - - - - - - - -

MATTHEW 7:7

**Ask, and it shall be given you; seek, and ye shall find;
knock, and it shall be opened unto you.**

Matthew – Lesson 5

MATTHEW 6:33

But seek ye first the kingdom of God,
and his righteousness; and all these things
shall be added unto you.

Matthew – Lesson 6

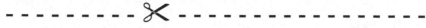

ROMANS 10:9

That if you confess with your mouth the Lord Jesus
and believe in your heart that God has raised
Him from the dead, you will be saved.   (NKJV)

Matthew – Lesson 7

ROMANS 12:2

And be not conformed to this world: but be ye
transformed by the renewing of your mind, that ye
may prove what is that good, and acceptable,
and perfect, will of God.

Matthew – Lesson 8

PROVERBS 3:5-6

Trust in the LORD with all your heart, and lean not on your own understanding; [6] In all your ways acknowledge Him, and he shall direct your paths. *(NKJV)*

Matthew – Lesson 9

GENESIS 1:26

And God said, Let us make man in our image, after our likeness: and let them have dominion over the fish of the sea, and over the fowl of the air, and over the cattle, and over all the earth, and over every creeping thing that creepeth upon the earth.

Mark – PET Scripture

MATTHEW 28:18

All power is given unto me in heaven and in earth.

Mark – Lesson 1

LUKE 10:19

Behold, I give unto you power to tread on serpents and scorpions, and over all the power of the enemy: and nothing shall by any means hurt you.

Mark – Lesson 1

JOHN 1:12

But as many as received him, to them gave he power to become the sons of God, even to them that believe on His name.

Mark – Lesson 2

ROMANS 4:17

...God, who quickeneth [to make alive or revive] the dead, and calleth those things which be not as though they were.

Mark – Lesson 2

MARK 16:17-18

And these signs shall follow them that believe; In my name shall they cast out devils; they shall speak with new tongues; [18] They shall take up serpents; and if they drink any deadly thing, it shall not hurt them; they shall lay hands on the sick, and they shall recover.

Mark – Lesson 3

MARK 11:23-24

For verily I say unto you, That whosoever shall say unto this mountain, Be thou removed, and be thou cast into the sea; and shall not doubt in his heart, but shall believe that those things which he saith shall come to pass; he shall have whatsoever he saith. [24] Therefore I say unto you, What things soever ye desire, when ye pray, believe that ye receive them, and ye shall have them.

Mark – Lesson 3

ISAIAH 54:17

No weapon that is formed against thee shall prosper; and every tongue that shall rise against thee in judgment thou shalt condemn. This is the heritage of the servants of the Lord, and their righteousness is of me, saith the Lord.

Mark – Lesson 4

PSALM 121:1-2

I will lift up mine eyes unto the hills, from whence cometh my help. ² My help cometh from the Lord, which made heaven and earth.

Mark – Lesson 4

PSALM 61:1-2

Hear my cry, O God; attend unto my prayer. ² From the end of the earth will I cry unto thee, when my heart is overwhelmed: lead me to the rock that is higher than I.

Mark – Lesson 5

PSALM 105:14-15

He suffered no man to do them wrong: yea, he reproved kings for their sakes; ¹⁵ Saying, Touch not mine anointed, and do my prophets no harm.

Mark – Lesson 5

II CORINTHIANS 4:18

While we look not at the things which are seen,
but at the things which are not seen:
for the things which are seen are temporal;
but the things which are not seen are eternal.

Luke - PET Scripture

- ✂ -

PSALM 23:1

The LORD is my shepherd;
I shall not want.

Luke – Lesson 1

- ✂ -

I PETER 5:7

Casting all your care upon him;
for he careth for you.

Luke – Lesson 1

PHILIPPIANS 4:19

But my God shall supply all your need according
to his riches in glory by Christ Jesus.

Luke – Lesson 2

--------------------------------- ✂ ---------------------------------

I JOHN 5:14

And this is the confidence that we have
in him, that, if we ask any thing according
to his will, he heareth us:

Luke – Lesson 3

GALATIANS 6:9

And let us not be weary in well doing:
for in due season we shall reap,
if we faint not.

Luke – Lesson 4

PHILIPPIANS 4:6

Be careful for nothing; but in every thing
by prayer and supplication with thanksgiving
let your requests be made known unto God.

Luke – Lesson 5

------------------------------- -------------------------------

PHILIPPIANS 2:5

Let this mind be in you,
which was also in Christ Jesus:

Luke – Lesson 6

------------------------------- ✂ -------------------------------

JAMES 1:8

A double minded man is
unstable in all his ways.

Luke – Lesson 6

ISAIAH 26:3

Thou wilt keep him in perfect peace,
whose mind is stayed on thee:
because he trusteth in thee.

Luke – Lesson 7

PHILIPPIANS 4:7

And the peace of God, which passeth all
understanding, shall keep your hearts
and minds through Christ Jesus.

Luke – Lesson 7

II CORINTHIANS 10:4-5

(For the weapons of our warfare are not carnal, but mighty through God to the pulling down of strong holds;) [5] Casting down imaginations, and every high thing that exalteth itself against the knowledge of God, and bringing into captivity every thought to the obedience of Christ;

Luke – Lesson 8

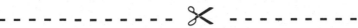

PHILIPPIANS 4:8

Finally, brethren, whatsoever things are true,
whatsoever things are honest,
whatsoever things are just,
whatsoever things are pure,
whatsoever things are lovely,
whatsoever things are of good report;
if there be any virtue,
and if there be any praise,
think on these things.

Luke – Lesson 8

II CORINTHIANS 5:17

Therefore if any man be in Christ, he is a new creature:
old things are passed away; behold,
all things are become new.

John - PET Scripture

- ✂ -

HEBREWS 11:1

Now faith is the substance of things hoped for,
the evidence of things not seen.

John – Lesson 1

HEBREWS 11:6

But without faith it is impossible to please him:
for he that cometh to God must believe that he is, and
that he is a rewarder of them that diligently seek him.

John – Lesson 2

ROMANS 10:17

So then faith cometh by hearing,
and hearing by the word of God.

John – Lesson 3

II CORINTHIANS 5:7

(For we walk by faith, not by sight:)

John – Lesson 4

GALATIANS 3:11

But that no man is justified by the law in
the sight of God, it is evident: for,
The just shall live by faith.

John – Lesson 5

PHILIPPIANS 3:13-14

Brethren, I count not myself to have apprehended: but this one thing I do, forgetting those things which are behind, and reaching forth unto those things which are before. [14] I press toward the mark for the prize of the high calling of God in Christ Jesus.

John – Lesson 6

EPHESIANS 4:22-24

That ye put off concerning the former conversation the old man, which is corrupt according to the deceitful lusts; [23] And be renewed in the spirit of your mind; [24] And that you put on the new man, which after God is created in righteousness and true holiness.

John – Lesson 7

PROVERBS 18:21

Death and life are in the power of the tongue: and they that love it shall eat the fruit thereof.

MATTHEW – PET SCRIPTURE

PSALM 1:2

But his delight is in the law of the Lord; and in his law doth he meditate day and night.

MATTHEW – LESSON 3

PHILIPPIANS 4:13

I can do all things through Christ who strengthens me.   (NKJV)

MATTHEW – LESSON 1

HOSEA 4:6

My people are destroyed for lack of knowledge: because thou hast rejected knowledge, I will also reject thee, that thou shalt be no priest to me: seeing thou hast forgotten the law of thy God, I will also forget thy children.

MATTHEW – LESSON 4

JAMES 2:17

Even so faith, if it hath not works, is dead, being alone.

MATTHEW – LESSON 2

MATTHEW 7:7

Ask, and it shall be given you; seek, and ye shall find; knock, and it shall be opened unto you.

MATTHEW – LESSON 5

MATTHEW 6:33

But seek ye first the kingdom of God, and his righteousness; and all these things shall be added unto you.

MATTHEW – LESSON 6

PROVERBS 3:5-6

Trust in the Lord with all your heart, and lean not on your own understanding; In all your ways acknowledge Him, and he shall direct your paths.
(NKJV)

MATTHEW – LESSON 9

ROMANS 10:9

That if you confess with your mouth the Lord Jesus and believe in your heart that God has raised Him from the dead, you will be saved.
(NKJV)

MATTHEW – LESSON 7

ROMANS 12:2

And be not conformed to this world: but be ye transformed by the renewing of your mind, that ye may prove what is that good, and acceptable, and perfect, will of God.

MATTHEW – LESSON 8

GENESIS 1:26

And God said, Let us make man in our image, after our likeness: and let them have dominion over the fish of the sea, and over the fowl of the air, and over the cattle, and over all the earth, and over every creeping thing that creepeth upon the earth.

MARK - PET SCRIPTURE

JOHN 1:12

But as many as received him, to them gave he power to become the sons of God, even to them that believe on His name.

MARK - LESSON 2

MATTHEW 28:18

All power is given unto me in heaven and in earth.

MARK – LESSON 1

ROMANS 4:17

…God, who quickeneth [to make alive or revive] the dead, and calleth those things which be not as though they were.

MARK - LESSON 2

LUKE 10:19

Behold, I give unto you power to tread on serpents and scorpions, and over all the power of the enemy: and nothing shall by any means hurt you.

MARK - LESSON 1

MARK 16:17-18

And these signs shall follow them that believe; In my name shall they cast out devils; they shall speak with new tongues; They shall take up serpents; and if they drink any deadly thing, it shall not hurt them; they shall lay hands on the sick, and they shall recover.

MARK – LESSON 3

MARK 11:23-24

For verily I say unto you, That whosoever shall say unto this mountain, Be thou removed, and be thou cast into the sea; and shall not doubt in his heart, but shall believe that those things which he saith shall come to pass; he shall have whatsoever he saith. Therefore I say unto you, What things soever ye desire, when ye pray, believe that ye receive them, and ye shall have them.

MARK – LESSON 3

PSALM 61:1-2

Here my cry, O God; attend unto my prayer. From the end of the earth will I cry unto thee when my heart is overwhelmed: lead me to the rock that is higher than I.

MARK - LESSON 5

ISAIAH 54:17

No weapon that is formed against thee shall prosper; and every tongue that shall rise against thee in judgment thou shalt condemn. This is the heritage of the servants of the Lord, and their righteousness is of me, saith the Lord.

MARK – LESSON 4

PSALM 105:14-15

He suffered no man to do them wrong: yea, he reproved kings for their sakes; Saying, Touch not mine anointed and do my prophets no harm.

MARK - LESSON 5

PSALM 121:1-2

I will lift up mine eyes unto the hills, from whence cometh my help. My help cometh from the Lord, which made heaven and earth.

MARK - LESSON 4

II CORINTHIANS 4:18

While we look not at the things which are seen, but at the things which are not seen: for the things which are seen are temporal; but the things which are not seen are eternal.

LUKE – PET SCRIPTURE

PHILIPPIANS 4:19

But my God shall supply all your need according to his riches in glory by Christ Jesus.

LUKE – LESSON 2

PSALM 23:1

The LORD is my shepherd; I shall not want.

LUKE – LESSON 1

I JOHN 5:14

And this is the confidence that we have in him, that, if we ask any thing according to his will, he heareth us:

LUKE – LESSON 3

I PETER 5:7

Casting all your care upon him; for he careth for you.

LUKE – LESSON 1

GALATIANS 6:9

And let us not be weary in well doing: for in due season we shall reap, if we faint not.

LUKE – LESSON 4

PHILIPPIANS 4:6

Be careful for nothing; but in every thing by prayer and supplication with thanksgiving let your requests be made known unto God.

LUKE – LESSON 5

ISAIAH 26:3

Thou wilt keep him in perfect peace, whose mind is stayed on thee: because he trusteth in thee.

LUKE – LESSON 7

PHILIPPIANS 2:5

Let this mind be in you, which was also in Christ Jesus:

LUKE – LESSON 6

PHILIPPIANS 4:7

And the peace of God, which passeth all understanding, shall keep your hearts and minds through Christ Jesus.

LUKE – LESSON 7

JAMES 1:8

A double minded man is unstable in all his ways.

LUKE – LESSON 6

II CORINTHIANS 10:4-5

(For the weapons of our warfare are not carnal, but mighty through God to the pulling down of strong holds;) Casting down imaginations, and every high thing that exalteth itself against the knowledge of God, and bringing into captivity every thought to the obedience of Christ;

LUKE – LESSON 8

PHILIPPIANS 4:8

Finally, brethren, whatsoever things are true, whatsoever things are honest, whatsoever things are just, whatsoever things are pure, whatsoever things are lovely, whatsoever things are of good report; if there be any virtue, and if there be any praise, think on these things.

LUKE – LESSON 8

II CORINTHIANS 5:17

Therefore if any man be in Christ, he is a new creature: old things are passed away; behold, all things are become new.

JOHN – PET SCRIPTURE

ROMANS 10:17

So then faith cometh by hearing, and hearing by the word of God.

JOHN – LESSON 3

HEBREWS 11:1

Now faith is the substance of things hoped for, the evidence of things not seen.

JOHN – LESSON 1

II CORINTHIANS 5:7

(For we walk by faith, not by sight:)

JOHN – LESSON 4

HEBREWS 11:6

But without faith it is impossible to please him: for he that cometh to God must believe that he is, and that he is a rewarder of them that diligently seek him.

JOHN – LESSON 2

GALATIANS 3:11

But that no man is justified by the law in the sight of God, it is evident: for, The just shall live by faith.

JOHN – LESSON 5

PHILIPPIANS 3:13-14

Brethren, I count not myself to have apprehended: but this one thing I do, forgetting those things which are behind, and reaching forth unto those things which are before. I press toward the mark for the prize of the high calling of God in Christ Jesus.

JOHN – LESSON 6

EPHESIANS 4:22-24

That ye put off concerning the former conversation the old man, which is corrupt according to the deceitful lusts; And be renewed in the spirit of your mind; And that you put on the new man, which after God is created in righteousness and true holiness.

JOHN – LESSON 7

About the Authors

Douglas M. Vincent

Douglas M. Vincent was born in Washington, DC and attended the University of the District of Columbia. After finding God in a time of personal chaos, Vincent dedicated his life to helping hurt and lost souls find their way to God. His desire is to direct them towards the Word, so that they will be more equipped to walk in God's plan for their lives. Vincent believes a vigorous study of the Gospel of Christ lays the groundwork for becoming an effective and mature Christian. He uses this workbook in ministering to those who want to establish a firm foundation in the Word of God. His desire is that *Achieving Intimacy With Jesus Christ* will be a blessing to all who seek a closer relationship with the Savior.

Judith E. Simms

Judith E. Simms, a native of Washington D.C., is a minister and teacher of the Gospel of Jesus Christ. Minister Simms received a Bachelor's of Science in Business Administration and has served in several capacities within the body of Christ. Her passion, however, lies in ministering to youth and young adults. Her firm belief that we must seek God daily for knowledge, understanding and wisdom, is what prompted her collaboration on *Achieving Intimacy With Jesus Christ*. Minister Simms has learned the importance of turning first to the one who guides and directs our paths. She also believes that the key to a stronger relationship with Christ begins with a fervent study of the Word of God. Minister Simms is often asked "How do you really get to know Jesus Christ?" She often responds, "Well, to know Him is to know His Word. Plain and simple."